TOO BUSY TO SHOP

Marketing to "Multi-Minding" Women

Kelley Murray Skoloda

Foreword by Geraldine Laybourne

Westport, Connecticut
London

Library of Congress Cataloging-in-Publication Data

Skoloda, Kelley Murray, 1964–
  Too busy to shop : marketing to "multi-minding" women /
Kelley Murray Skoloda ; foreword by Geraldine Laybourne.
    p. cm.
  Includes bibliographical references and index.
  ISBN 978-0-313-35487-8 (alk. paper)
  1. Women consumers. 2. Marketing. I. Title.
  HC79.C6S57   2009
  658.8'34082—dc22   2008041034

British Library Cataloguing in Publication Data is available.

Library of Congress Catalog Card Number: 2008041034
ISBN: 978-0-313-35487-8

First published in 2009

Praeger Publishers, 88 Post Road West, Westport, CT 06881
An imprint of Greenwood Publishing Group, Inc.
www.praeger.com

Printed in the United States of America

The paper used in this book complies with the
Permanent Paper Standard issued by the National
Information Standards Organization (Z39.48–1984).

10 9 8 7 6 5 4 3 2 1

Copyright Acknowledgments

Multi-minding[SM] is a registered service mark of Ketchum
Worldwide. All Rights Reserved.

To David, who makes me think anything is possible.
To Jake, Ellie, and my family for their love and support.

Contents

Foreword

I met Kelley Skoloda several years ago when we were working on Oxygen Network's Mentors Walk, an event that showed prominent women in the world walking and talking, advising, and encouraging the next generation of young women. She engaged me immediately at that event and does so again in this book with her powerful idea: Women are much more than multi-taskers; we are *multi-minders*.

Her thoughts connect with the work of anthropologist Helen Fisher on the structure of women's brains. In a nutshell (forgive me, Helen): men's brains are bigger (you have to say that first or you men out there won't listen to the rest), but women have 12 percent more prefrontal cortex. This prefrontal cortex enables us to process multiple thoughts at once ... it is the connective tissue that allows us to talk about world peace, Swiffers, kindergarten enrollment, and business plans all in the same paragraph. It really is our blessing and our curse. It is why we drive men crazy and why we make great strategic thinkers.

Kelley, a preeminent marketer to women, takes the idea of *multi-mindedness* and dissects what this means to any business that wants to thrive in the twenty-first century. She packs this book with powerful statistics, case studies, and *must-do* lists, all backed by her innate common sense.

Her statistics back up what we all know instinctively—women buy just about everything today. I spent the first 16 years of my career building Nickelodeon and convincing marketers about the important influence of kids and the next 10 years focusing on the importance of women as consumers. In many ways, it was easier to get marketers to take kids seriously, probably because their power is somewhat limited and women's power is limitless.

It struck me as we would talk about the wide-ranging influence of women (cars, houses, technology, you name it) that men were usually the first to get it: "That's right, my wife buys everything." Yet, they weren't prepared to make wholesale changes in the way their companies thought of women as their prime customers. At best, they would have "niche" approaches within their organizations.

This book has the most compelling set of statistics. We need to put these in every presentation we make. Clearly, we need to put these facts in front of marketers relentlessly and often.

Women are tough customers, and Kelley tells you that in song and verse. Why wouldn't marketers understand that to solve the equation of growing sales, they must focus everything on designing, marketing, and selling to women? Men, in a sense, are low-hanging fruit. Tell them it's fast and cool and you've got them. It is why we love them, but they only buy 15 percent of all consumer goods and services.

This is a primer for growing your business, but it is not simplistic. It calls for a rethinking of how you know your customers; how and where you market; how you connect on a values level (you can't just *say*, you have to *do*); the importance of making explicit the use of experts and process of product development; a consumer-versus-product orientation (don't just build it—we won't come unless you think about *us* first, and only then will we be loyal to your product); and what partnership really means.

One of the things I know for sure is that if you give us an emotional connection, we will be your sales reps for life. We will brag about your products to our friends, co-workers, and relatives. We really *are* looking for a commitment.

Geraldine Laybourne
Former Chief Executive Officer, Oxygen Network

Acknowledgments

You know those mental lists we all have of something we'd like to do some day? Well, I've always wanted to write a book. In fact, I've started several. But starting a book and finishing a book are two very different things.

The bridge between the two was actually saying out loud to someone that I wanted to write a book. That someone was David, my husband, who believes in me so much that he automatically just assumed it would happen and, from that day forward, encouraged me to add author to my roles of wife, mother, and professional. Thank you, David, for your love, support, encouragement, sense of humor, and extraordinary talent for playing with the kids. You are a wonderful husband and dad.

It truly astounded me that each time I told someone in my family, a friend, or a colleague about the book project, as I called it, they jumped on the bandwagon, offering advice, encouragement, and a suggestion for someone else I could talk to for help. I am truly blessed to have such a supportive network of family, friends, and colleagues.

My gratitude goes to some special women—Dale Bornstein, Mimi Doe, Nan McCann, and Brenda Vester—who provided exceptional encouragement from the very beginning. Thanks for telling me I could do it. My good friends Merry, DeAnn, Nanette, and Joanne and my cousin, Renea, were great at asking, "How's the book going?" at just the right time. Nana and Pappy, thank you for your interest and your sense of humor.

Every person I interviewed was excited, accessible, and supportive. My thanks go to Marti Barletta, Mark Baynes, Dale Bornstein, JoAnne Boyle, Gay Browne, Kassie Canter, Carol Cone, Emilio Cornacchione, Denis Darragh, Stacy DeBroff, Mimi Doe, Amy Keroes, Geraldine Laybourne, Hedy Lukas, Susan Molinari, Leslie Morgan Steiner, Paul Rand, Janet Riccio, and Rich Tavoletti.

Tracy Carbasho provided invaluable editing support. Thanks, Tracy.

Big thank-yous go to all of the women who encouraged and partici-pated in my blog, www.toobusytoshop.blogspot.com. It was a pleasure and privilege to connect with you.

My colleagues at Ketchum have been inspirational and I so appreci-ate their encouragement and help. Thanks to Maegen Noble, Courtney Murphy, Linda Eatherton, Gur Tsabar, Ray Kotcher, Kristen Laney, Linda Schuler, Deanne Yamamoto, Sue Maloney, Karen Strauss, Barri Rafferty, Serena DeMorgan, Allison Costello, Ron Culp, Pamela Von Lehmden, Dave Chapman, Carmine Gallo, Mindy Rubinstein, Robyn Massey, Josh Shabtai, and everyone else who gave me advice, pointed me in a good direction, asked how I was doing, or gave me their two cents' worth.

Two special men, Larry Werner and Jerry Voros, have been mentors throughout my entire career. In fact, they enabled me to start my career. Without them, I would not be where I am today. Thank you from the bottom of my heart.

Jeff Olson at Praeger Publishers sent me a note years ago that helped to inspire the writing of this book. Thank you, Jeff.

My mom and my sister have been constant sources of support. I could not do what I do without the two of you. You are strong, smart, good women, and I admire you both more than you know. My dad, a former drill instructor in the Marine Corps who is no longer here, gave me a strong sense of self-discipline that has served me well throughout my life. My brothers are constant sources of humor. Nonnie and Pap, you are here in spirit. Thank you.

Jake and Ellie, you are the joys of my life and wonderful sources of encouragement. Jake, you went along with the writing of this book just like it was a perfectly normal thing to do. I love that you have written your own book and are planning to write more. Thank you for choosing the colors for my blog.

Ellie, I love the book you wrote about animals. As you sat in your office under my desk, sent me love notes written in crayon, combed my hair into ponytails, and told me "Mommy, it's time to play now" (all while I was writing), you inspired me to be a good author and an even better mom.

Introduction

It seems that everywhere you turn in the communications and marketing world, the topic of marketing to women is red hot. In all of the 20-plus years I have spent in the communications industry, I have never seen such interest in the topic. It is unprecedented. Headlines tout the power of the woman's purse. Major marketers refer to their customers as "her." Female-focused consultancies are being launched by businesses ranging from freelancers to the largest of communications companies. A movement is in progress. Today, almost every business wants, and in fact needs, to reach women.

In truth, it is really no wonder that marketing to women has become a priority for marketers and business owners. Women make 85 percent of consumer purchasing decisions, spending more than $3.3 trillion annually. The business interest in marketing to women will only continue to grow as women's buying power escalates. Attracting their purchasing power is no longer a "nice to do"—it is a "must-do." What is astonishing to me is not that the marketing-to-women revolution is here, but rather that this movement did not start sooner.

While this unprecedented buying power is driving marketers' attention more than ever before, current efforts are not working as well as they would like. But why? For one, women are "multi-minding"—more on that in a moment—making them more difficult to reach than ever.

Based on the constantly increasing influence of female consumers in the marketplace, my experiences with major clients and prospects, and many personal conversations with thought leaders in the communications industry, it is clear that market demand for information on how to reach women is outpacing the amount of resources currently available.

There is a growing body of work on the topics, but none of the current offerings address the single, pervasive phenomenon that explains what is happening, which applies to businesses ranging from the local hair salon to megabrands. *Too Busy to Shop* unveils the concept of multi-minding and explains its important implications to marketers.

Why is the market demanding a new approach? Women have bypassed multi-tasking and are multi-minding. Multi-minding, in a nutshell, means constantly juggling myriad thoughts and tasks to manage the many dimensions and responsibilities of a woman's life. This definition will come into focus as you read.

Multi-minding has become a survival technique for those living busy lives. Given that women are choosing to live robust, activity-filled lives, this coping mechanism is not likely to go away. In fact, it likely will continue at an accelerated pace. Multi-minding is a real cultural phenomenon, and it is here to stay.

The term multi-minding, coined during my work at Ketchum, the global public relations firm, has already received significant attention in the trade and business media. Many times when I have explained the concept to female marketers, media, or friends and family, they say, "That's me! You have just described my life." Multi-minding is not a trend; it is a reality of women's lives.

I have talked with dozens of marketers and hundreds of women. Marketers and business owners still wrestle every day with the most effective ways to reach women, especially in this age of digital change. Marketers, ranging from the most sophisticated to new entrants, have intense interest in the topic and are actively seeking solutions to better reach female consumers. Women want marketers to help them solve problems, not just to receive commercial messages.

What is particularly important to marketers about multi-minding is that multi-minding means women have little time for commercial messages. That means we must find better, more effective ways to reach female consumers. This book will explain how to do just that.

Too Busy to Shop is based on research, interviews with experts in the fields of marketing and branding, and my own understanding of the women's market, based on leading-edge work in brand marketing with major clients in a global public relations firm. As a partner and director of Global Brand Marketing Practice at Ketchum, I have counseled many clients and spoken dozens of times on the topics of multi-minding and marketing to women. The work that my teams and I have done while at Ketchum has been featured in *BusinessWeek* online, *BRANDWEEK* magazine, *Fast Company* magazine, *PINK Magazine*, *CNNMoney.com*, and many other online and print news outlets.

Over the course of a 20-year career in marketing and public relations, I have been fortunate to work with some of the biggest and most highly regarded brands and companies in the world, ranging from technology and television networks to cereal and cleaning products. I have been extremely lucky to have met and worked with some of the smartest and most insightful experts in the marketing world today. A number of them have become wonderful professional friends.

Through this vast array of experiences and exposure to exceptional people, I have access to information, trends, and insights that have collectively contributed a great deal to the content in this book. In essence, this book provides you with that same access to information, experiences, and great minds that you otherwise would not have.

Much like news show hosts who track news and then facilitate a dialogue with experts, I will share consumer research, explore real, successful examples, and interview masterminds in the business. And, I will share insights and input from real women, who have some pretty good advice for you.

As I interviewed experts and women, I was constantly amazed at the willingness and enthusiasm, in fact downright passion, for the topic and for sharing perspectives. From chief marketing officers to work-at-home moms, my requests for input were embraced with a "yes!" followed by effusive commentary. Each and every interview was lively, information-filled, and fun. I hope those feelings come through loud and clear as you read each chapter.

So, how do marketers tap into women's complex multi-minding state of mind? You have taken a good first step by buying this book. Now read it. You'll get behind-the-scenes examples of effective connections with multi-minding women, analyzed by some of the master minds in the business today.

Unlike other marketing-to-women books, readers get how-tos and action items, packaged as "M^2 Must-Dos" (M^2 = multi-minding) and based on insiders' views into some of the most successful marketing-to-women campaigns of recent times. Each chapter also concludes with "Questions Every Marketer or Business Owner Should Ask." These elements will reinforce key concepts and prompt you to action.

If you are looking for a single, magic bullet, you will have to keep looking. As many studies and even more anecdotal stories prove, women are not single-focus creatures. This book reflects a holistic approach that resonates with women—a blueprint, if you will, for a better way to reach female consumers. It cites examples that will help you build your own initiatives from the blueprint. As with any successful relationship, it is a journey, not a destination.

I hope you join me on this journey, which leads to new and better ways to market to women. The rulebook is being written as we speak. Will your brand or business be a part of it? It is worth it to be included. To lag behind and to do less with today's powerful, techno-savvy, multi-minding female consumer will eventually erode your bottom line.

If you have a vested interest in marketing to women—and what business doesn't?—read on.

Chapter One

Staggering Stats: Buying Power of the Female Consumer

> Forget multi-tasking—women like Varma are "multi-minding," a newly coined buzz phrase that describes the process of simultaneously thinking about various things.
>
> —Gogoi in *BusinessWeek* online (2005)

In the future, when multi-minding women are too busy to shop, the parking lots at malls may be nearly empty and the visits to many branded Web sites may slow to a trickle. Sound farfetched?

Well, female consumers who are constantly juggling the many dimensions of their lives, or multi-minding, have less time for purely commercial messages. These women have little time to shop in the traditional sense—browsing and serving as a one-way receiver of marketing messages. However, they still need and want to buy, especially since they are the primary buyers for the majority of goods and services.

In the time it's taken you to read this far, today's busy woman has already achieved what I will initially call "it." In fact, research indicates that most women do it at least 10 times every five minutes.

What exactly is "it?" It is multi-minding, or simultaneously managing numerous aspects of an increasingly busy lifestyle. I think that is why the *BusinessWeek* reporter, Pallavi Gogoi, proclaimed that multi-tasking is passé and multi-minding is the new phrase. As mothers, wives, employees, and chief purchasing officers for families, most women today live and breathe multi-minding.

Multi-tasking has evolved and women are now accustomed to addressing a complex mix of family, career, and self-care decisions at any given moment with little time to shop in the traditional sense. However, these women are still the primary buyers of goods and services in the United States, making it imperative for companies to pay attention to this trend.

According to the seminal research on multi-minding conducted by the global public relations firm Ketchum, 61 percent of women in general, and 62 percent of women ages 25 to 54, say they have little time for commercial messages.[1] That dynamic means we need to find better and different ways to reach these busy and powerful consumers.

Even if today's woman appears to be relaxing in front of a late-night television show, reading a magazine in the pediatrician's office, or tackling a complicated analytical study at work, she is probably also thinking about and preparing for the other dimensions of her life. Perhaps she is weighing the benefits of her 401(k) plan, plotting out her organic vegetable garden, ticking off birthday party logistics, and longing for a neck massage.

Kris, a busy mom with three children and a part-time job, is an ideal example of a woman who represents a marketer's dream, but also a marketer's biggest challenge. I recently sat in yet another conference room in Chicago with a group of smart, experienced marketing executives who are struggling to connect with Kris and female consumers like her who have never wielded as much power in the marketplace as they do now.

When Kris is home, she usually has the television turned on. However, she is barely able to watch whatever program is on and is subconsciously filtering out the commercials. She is too busy preparing three different lunches, making a call about her work schedule for the next day, mentally checking off things that need to be done in preparation for a birthday party, and letting the barking dog back inside. Today's time-challenged women have to engage in constant multi-minding, which means they have little or no time for commercial messages.

Meanwhile, our executives back in Chicago admit their television advertising is not working the way it used to, even though it is still a mainstay in their marketing toolkit. They are unsure about how to connect with women like Kris in a relevant and effective way. I believe companies must find creative ways to reach Kris and millions of other women. If not, the parking lots at malls may be nearly empty and the traffic to many branded Web sites may slow to a trickle in the future.

GET READY FOR A BIG CHANGE

Over the next 10 years, the way women buy their products and services will change dramatically. For example, they will buy brands and patronize businesses that exude credibility, quickly connect with them, communicate to them in a 360-degree fashion where they live (physically and online), and sustain a consistent relationship with them. In-home shopping, both online and offline, will save precious time. Successful brands will engage with women in such a way that they will share the management of the brand with consumers. In short, female consumers not only will drive the majority of purchases, but also will build and manage the marketing.

Hard to believe, but not surprising, if you know that today's women have emerged as a more powerful consumer force than ever before and they have changing expectations of marketers.

WOMEN ARE NOT A NICHE MARKET

In the United States, women now control $3.3 trillion in consumer spending, are responsible for more than 80 percent of the household buying, control more than 50 percent of the wealth in the country, make 62 percent of all car purchases, and take more than 50 percent of all business trips.[2] Yet, many marketers fail to recognize and reach them fully, still treating women as part of a niche demographic, rather than major drivers of purchasing decisions.

In fact, I was just in a meeting the other day when a chief executive officer (CEO) of a fairly progressive company asked me if a focus on women was too "niched."

"Will we risk ignoring other audiences if we market to women?" the CEO wondered. "What about all of those young guys you read about who are so hard to reach through traditional advertising. Aren't we overlooking them?"

Well, there are certain product and service categories, such as video gaming systems, flat-screen televisions, and pizza delivery, where men, indeed, are the primary purchasers. In those cases, a clear focus on men or a subsegment of men makes perfect sense. Women, however, are the purchase decision makers for 85 percent of the household spending. Therefore, if we are talking about food, toys, durable goods, consumer-packaged goods, health care, baby products, clothing, books, cars, consumer electronics, homes, and many other categories, women currently are or are fast becoming the primary purchasers.

With those statistics, I think the CEO is asking the wrong questions. It is not the first time I have been asked that very same question and I am sure it will not be the last. The "niche" focus that he and other executives are concerned about is, in fact, the primary consumer for many brands and businesses. Clearly, there is a need to understand the enormous and growing buying power that women have today.

According to a *BusinessWeek* magazine special report on female consumer buying power, women pack a one-two punch of purchasing power and decision-making authority. Although women typically earn only 78 cents for every dollar men make, they are responsible for more than 80 percent of the buying decisions.[3]

There is a massive disconnect between this compelling information and the questions asked by the CEO. Therefore, it is not surprising that one of the questions I am often asked when I speak at conferences is "How do I sell this to my senior management?" Many senior managers somehow think marketing to women will take the focus away from another target group.

Take a look at these revealing stats, provided by the M2W Conference, the largest marketing-to-women event in the country.[4] Women account for the following:

* 85 percent of all consumer purchases, ranging from cars to computers
* 91 percent of new homes
* 66 percent of personal computers
* 92 percent of vacations
* 80 percent of health care decisions
* 65 percent of new cars
* 89 percent of bank accounts
* 93 percent of food purchases
* 93 percent of over-the-counter pharmaceuticals

Indeed, marketing to women does change what is done in the marketing mix because women process information and make purchasing decisions differently than men. Unfortunately, the current marketing in many product categories is missing the mark. Consider these statistics:[5]

* 59 percent of women feel misunderstood by food marketers.
* 66 percent of women feel misunderstood by health care marketers.
* 74 percent of women feel misunderstood by automotive marketers.
* 84 percent of women feel misunderstood by investment marketers.
* 70 percent of new businesses are started by women.

WOMEN BUY SOAP AND SERVERS

More businesses are being started by women and more households are being headed by women than ever before—27 percent, a fourfold increase since 1950—which is partially responsible for the growth in the influence and purchasing power of women. In fact, today's American moms are the first to live in a time in which more women, (51 percent) are living without a spouse than with one. At the same time, women's median income has increased 63 percent compared with men's, which is essentially flat in that time period with growth of just 0.6 percent.[6]

Because women tend to take care of others' needs as well as their own, they typically buy for the members of their family, too. In addition, more women are also buying for their businesses. According to the Center for Women's Business Research, women-owned businesses have grown over the past two decades at twice the rate of all businesses, bringing the number of women-owned firms to more than 10 million, which represents massive buying power.[7] Don't forget that every woman business owner is also a consumer and many female consumers are, or will be, business owners.

According to *PINK Magazine*,

> It's no secret that women spend more than three trillion dollars a year on goods and services. What is relatively new is that women are now making key purchasing decisions for large B2B contracts. Translated, we may be choosing laundry detergent at night, but during the day we are deciding between a $30-million server farm from Dell or IBM.[8]

Tom Peters' book, *Re-Imagine! Business Excellence in a Disruptive Age* (2006), outlines the strong influence women have when purchasing products. In the book *Trends* (2005), co-authored by Peters and Marti Barletta, the first chapter stresses,

> But we must wake up and smell the truth: women are the primary purchasers of … damn near everything. We must, therefore, strive on every front to achieve nothing less than total enterprise realignment around this awesome, burgeoning, astoundingly untapped market.[9]

Peters notes, "Women are where it's at" when it comes to the tremendous, current purchasing power of female consumers. That trend is anticipated to grow. By 2010, women are expected to control $1 trillion, or 60 percent, of the country's wealth, according to research conducted by *BusinessWeek* and Gallup.

Barletta, a noted consultant and author of *Marketing to Women: How to Understand, Reach and Increase Your Share of the World's Largest Market Segment* (2003), believes women buy most of almost everything. "Just a few years ago, I always had to start my presentations with a fairly extensive overview of women's earning and buying power. These days, I don't. The research is clear; the numbers are huge," Barletta concludes. More CEOs need a visit from Barletta.

I have seen compelling examples of marketing that seem to be succeeding with multi-minding women of varying ages. As women's tremendous buying power is growing in both traditionally female areas, like consumer-packaged goods, and in traditionally male-dominated areas, like do-it-yourself products, financial services, and motorcycles, it is informative to review examples in each category. While dolls and motorcycles are very different categories, smart companies in both markets are successfully turning the heads of multi-minding women.

TRADITIONAL PRODUCT CATEGORIES CAN STILL RESONATE
WITH MULTI-MINDING WOMEN

Let's start with a product that has been marketed to generations of women for more than 40 years, the Barbie doll. From princess to president, Barbie has a multitude of jobs and corresponding marketing campaigns. Remember the Barbie and Ken breakup? It made headlines worldwide. Barbie was the world's doll, a celebrity in her own right.

No matter what your personal opinion of Barbie may be, you have to admit she has captured her fair share of attention over the years. She seemed to have a place in almost every girl's home until she was upstaged by a number of doll lines that were marketed as much trendier versions of the ubiquitous doll.

While Barbie and Bratz dolls both sport cosmetics, a dizzying array of fashions, and as many friends as a social networking site, there was a distinct difference. Barbie clearly maintained a "good girl" image, full of girly aspirations, fairies, and good, clean fun. The others proudly displayed the opposite, a rebellious "bad girl," complete with all of the trappings of the darker side of celebrity. Think Jennifer Aniston versus Britney Spears. You get the picture.

Girls were drawn to the glittery make-up, au courant fashions, and trendy hairstyles of the "new dolls on the street." Mothers bought them and let their daughters buy them. Barbie was losing her throne.

The marketers at Mattel, makers of Barbie, must have racked their brains wondering how to make Barbie more relevant to girls and the audience who most often purchases the dolls, their moms. Their inventive and smart solution, the We Believe in Girls initiative, combines authenticity in a way that is really resonating with multi-minding women.

Clothes, hairstyle, footwear, and popular activities are all subject to current trends. The underlying personality of the dolls, though, was a constant. That is where Barbie succeeded in creating an idea that could appeal to women that, while on trend, was timeless in its appeal—Barbie's belief in girls and the importance of preserving girlhood.

The We Believe in Girls Web site says it best:

> We believe in girls. In their dreams. And in their very natural, built-in desire to change the world.
> We believe in playtime (and more of it).
> We believe, in fact, that the magic of a happy, playful, inspired girlhood is the same secret ingredient that creates happy, inspired and powerful women.
> And the world could use as many of those as possible, right?[10]

The mission goes on to talk about the pressures resident in our culture, like those associated with cosmetics and clothing, that force girls to grow up too soon. The marketers at Mattel know that girls today are growing up faster than ever before. Girls face a barrage of messages, mainly from the media, about their outward appearance and sexuality. Mothers, fathers, and anyone who cares about girls would like to preserve a safe and healthy girlhood, and tapping into this psyche is a smart way to make the brand relevant and to supersede the clutter of commercial product messages, especially with multi-minding women.

The Web site continues, "Our goal is to invite and facilitate the conversation. Everyone is invited to participate, from moms and dads to teachers, academics, and behaviorists—anyone who cares about girls' well-being."[11]

Striking up a "conversation" is a smart and effective way to engage multi-minding women. These women have little time for commercial messages, but this conversation on a topic they care deeply about transcends commercial messages. The message affects them, their families, and their daily lives. In short, it is a message that quickly connects.

The We Believe initiative succeeds in other areas that are important to multi-minding women, as well. The messages are delivered by messengers that female consumers consider to be credible—women and mothers. A revolving advisory panel of experts was established to provide guidance and direction for the We Believe mission. It will "provide an internationally diverse point of view, focused on what's happening now and what's next for girls and girlhood around the world. Long term, the advisory council will serve as a sounding board for philanthropic and nonprofit initiatives—including scholarships and endowments."[12]

For instance, Leslie Morgan Steiner, author of *Mommy Wars* (2006), served as an initial expert to help launch the program. Other advisors include doctors, psychologists, authors, and parenting experts.

There is "heft" to the initiative in terms of looking at this issue globally. A 2007 research report prepared by MME Research, *Global Media Coverage of Tween Girls*, determined how local media around the world covered the subject of girls, including their maturity and self-esteem, and analyzed how the treatment of the subjects differed from region to region. What was the key finding? Overall, they found that regardless of the region, girls are under enormous pressure, whether it is simply to survive amid great poverty or to live up to conflicting societal standards.[13]

The research did not stop there. *The Worldwide Mom & Daughter Survey* (2007) was commissioned in partnership with Cheryl Dellasega, Ph.D., author of numerous books on issues affecting women. This survey of 2,000 moms with daughters between the ages of 6 and 12 explores regional similarities and differences in how mothers provide for their daughters. The research will explore what contributes to a happy and healthy girlhood.

Wow. Here is credibility in the form of messages that quickly connect and a commitment to ongoing activities, all connected to something
that really matters to the consumer. Now that is a success in the making
with multi-minding women. I predict these women will make time to
shop for Barbie.

I see those empty parking lots at the mall with a few more cars in
them now … or will there be more motorcycles in those lots?

MULTI-MINDING WOMEN DRIVING FUTURE MOTORCYCLE SALES

American women are the fastest-growing part of the motorcycle
business, buying more than 100,000 bikes a year. A recent *New York
Times* article on the topic of marketing motorcycles to women notes,
"Even though aging baby-boomer men, with money to spend and time
on their hands, have played a big role in expanding the market in
recent years, motorcycle companies are trying hard to woo women
buyers."[14]

Harley-Davidson, like other companies that have not traditionally
marketed their products to women, is now recognizing the powerful
buying potential of women. According to the company's data, women
represent 1 in 10 U.S. motorcycle riders and account for nearly 12 percent of new Harley-Davidson motorcycle purchases.[15]

What is happening here? Marketing motorcycles, and not just any
motorcycle, but marketing Harleys to women?

Interestingly, it seems that Harley is doing more than any other
motorcycle company in terms of product development. On the product
front, Harley is producing more motorcycles with narrow seats that are
lower to the ground than traditional models to make them more
comfortable for women. The company is also "selling more clothes in
bright colors and with rhinestones, rather than the standard-issue black-
and-orange leather jackets. Even the skull motif that appears on some
clothing sold at Harley outlets has undergone a friendly makeover to
include wings and flowers," according to the *New York Times*.[16]

Undoubtedly, clothes capture the attention of many women, but it
takes more than fashion flair to reach multi-minding women. That is
where Harley and other motorcycle companies are at a distinct disad-
vantage. They need to sell a relatively new and expensive category to
women, in addition to building a brand preference. They will have to
build a network of interested women, not just tap into one that exists
for categories that have already built relationships with women.

Harley is ramping up its efforts on the very-important-to-women
communications front. Car dealers take note: Harley dealers have sought
the advice of experts in selling to female consumers so that the showroom
experience is more female friendly. Also at the retail level, dealers hold
garage parties to educate women about bikes. This party idea should

Questions Every Marketer or Business Owner Should Ask

- Who is currently buying most of my products or services? Who will present the biggest buying opportunities in the future?
- What local or national cause or issue might be a good match for my company or brand? Have I asked the opinions of those who buy my products or services?
- How can I engage or more actively engage consumers in a way that helps them and transcends commercialism?
- How am I letting my consumers know that I hear them and I am changing based on their input?

work well with multi-minding women who can learn about something new (motorcycles) and get together with their girlfriends at the same time.

Another must-do when trying to reach multi-minding women is providing detailed information online so they can conduct an Internet search when it is convenient for them. The company smartly added a "Women & Motorcycling" section on its Web site for female bikers with tips on appropriate gear and how to ride safely. Though not readily apparent when you enter the main Harley-Davidson site, the section also profiles female riders and promotes the garage parties.

In 2007, for the first time, Harley-Davidson marketed to women at the Sturgis Motorcycle Rally, one of the most important motorcycle events in the country. The company launched a series of events specifically for women, including a kiosk for women-centric activities, as well as a women's day, which featured women-only demonstrations, seminars, and special guests.

Women at the event, most of whom attended with a spouse or boyfriend, saw for the first time that Harley was paying attention to them as female riders. Harley may not have a robust network of female riders, but the company gave credibility to its women's marketing efforts by addressing them at the Sturgis event, instead of at a separate women's event.

Harley-Davidson clearly has more work to do if the company truly wants to succeed in attracting female consumers to the category and the brand. However, if the efforts so far are any indication, the company should succeed over time in claiming a leadership position in marketing motorcycles to women.

MULTI-MINDING IS HERE TO STAY

Whether your brand has been marketed to women for decades or you are just starting to market less traditional products to women, you will have to deal with the dynamic of multi-minding in women's lives today. This book will explore multi-minding and its major implications for marketers. Through expert opinions and case studies, you will more fully understand the multi-minding phenomenon and how to engage women for your brand or business.

Please remember, there is no silver bullet or a one-stop-shop answer about how to more effectively engage women. It is an ongoing process, a journey. Think of it as you would if you were building an important relationship. It is something you live, day in and day out, not something you check off your to-do list.

The effort is well worth it. Without women buying your product or service, chances are good that you will not have a product or service to sell in the future.

M^2 Must-Dos

- ✓ Realize the purchasing power of the female consumer today and change your marketing to reflect that focus.
- ✓ Use compelling statistics about the marketplace to sell-in marketing-to-women to senior management.
- ✓ Connect an iconic brand to a relevant social issue that will enable product messages to transcend commercialism.
- ✓ Engage consumers in your social issue marketing, make changes based on their input, commit to financial and nonfinancial support, and consistently communicate about your activities.
- ✓ Create an advisory panel of experts and real women to react to marketing campaigns, test products, and serve as a sounding board—giving them a vested interest in your business.

Chapter Two

The Apple of Many Eyes: Women Buyers Now Getting More Attention from Marketers

Jane, a working mother with two children, can sum up how she feels about marketing messages with one word: bombarded.

"It's not just magazines, TV, radio, direct mail, and billboards any more. Now, add Web sites, e-mail, blogs, in-home parties, schools, parks, stadiums, and many more to the mix. It seems like every marketer in the world wants my attention," says Jane. "Now, on top of everything else I have to juggle in my life, I have to wade through and manage all of these external messages."

Jane is right. There is more room for marketing today with the proliferation of media, including more than 200 cable networks, nearly 5,500 consumer magazines, 10,500 radio stations, millions of Web sites, and more than 100 million blogs. Couple that with the influential buying power of the female consumer and it is no wonder Jane is the apple of many marketers' eyes.

Some marketers, like food and consumer-packaged goods companies, have been marketing to women for a long time. With women's purchasing power extending to more nontraditional categories, like consumer electronics, cars, and do-it-yourself products, women are now getting much more attention from those marketers, too. Whether traditional or nontraditional, marketers of all shapes and sizes are increasingly trying to do more and better jobs at reaching the powerful female consumer.

REAL FOCUS ON MARKETING TO WOMEN RELATIVELY NEW

Given the compelling statistics on buying power, you would think marketing to women would be a studied and sophisticated arena that has been in place for a long time. In reality, the focus on trying to do it better is a relatively novel idea.

Believe it or not, the first national marketing-to-women conference, M2W, was launched just in 2005. This is quite surprising in light of the statistics that prove women have been the primary purchasers for their households for decades. If you are marketing to women and have not attended M2W, you should add it to your agenda of must-do activities.

Nan McCann is president of PME Enterprises, a Connecticut-based sales and marketing agency that organizes M2W and M2Moms, the largest marketing-to-women and marketing-to-moms conferences in the country. I talked with McCann about the initial impetus for the conferences, which companies she thinks are doing a good job, and what she predicts for the future of marketing to women.

In the early 2000s, we were doing a conference that focused on mature markets. The conferences revealed that women in the 50-plus age category were making almost all of the purchasing decisions. Whether it was housing, retirement living, health care, or gifts for grandchildren, women were driving the buying."

McCann continues, "In 2003, we started doing research to find out what conferences or educational opportunities existed on the topic of marketing to women in general. What we found was shocking. There was nothing there."

In light of the undeniable statistics on women's buying power, it seems logical that marketing to women would be a mainstream activity. Interestingly, though, even some of the leading marketing trade journals, like *BRANDWEEK* magazine, feature a yearly special section on marketing to women, as if marketing to women is still a niche.

MARKETING PLAYING CATCH UP WITH ECONOMIC POWER

"Women have been an amazing force in the American economy for decades. It was startling to us that women were not focused on as a compelling consumer force," McCann recalls. "In many of our preliminary conversations with major companies and brands, marketing to women was included under diversity marketing initiatives. They were not viewed as the mainstream force that they are."

Meanwhile on the business front, the first-ever national magazine for female executives, *PINK Magazine*, was launched in 2006. Two smart women, Cynthia Good and Genevieve Bos, founded *PINK* because they were well aware that women have been leading businesses for years, but there was never a national magazine to address their unique needs, interests, and ambitions. Women have been in the workforce in droves for decades, but addressing their needs as a driving force in the work world is in its infancy.

Also in 2006, marketing to women was covered for the first time as a stand-alone topic at the Public Relations Society of America's international conference. For the first time that same year, a panel discussion called "What Women Want, Connecting with the New Technology Consumer," was held at the massive Consumer Electronics Show and was devoted entirely to exploring the needs of female consumers.

Many women buyers are clearly getting more attention from marketers. Other significant marketplace developments emerged around that same time. For example, the terms "mommy blogger" and "alpha moms" entered our mainstream lexicon. McCann says that while she was talking to marketers about their efforts to communicate with women, she kept hearing requests for a conference that focused on moms. Just as there had been few diligent attempts to market to women in general, there was even less of an effort to reach moms.

"Some agencies and experts actually dissuaded us from doing a marketing-to-moms conference," McCann remembers. "They just did not think moms represented a lucrative enough business opportunity that marketers would want to pay attention to. That was a few, short years ago and today, women and moms are commanding headlines as the most lucrative groups."

McCann provides an interesting historical perspective:

In my seventh-grade American studies class in the 1960s, we were asked to write a short essay on what we'd become if we could be anything when we grew up. I said that I'd like to be president. A huge debate ensued with many children commenting that a woman would not be capable of such a job, but today we even have women who are moms running for the top offices in this country. Women and marketers have come a long way in a short time.

REAL AND VIRTUAL ECONOMIES DRIVEN BY WOMEN

Many working women, including McCann, were paid little in their first job. Women have rapidly progressed from those meager wages to being drivers of the economy and are on their way to becoming drivers of the virtual economy.

"Technology has skyrocketed our marketing capabilities," observes McCann. "Technology has enabled women to make different choices in life whether that's working from home or shopping from home. It's made a real difference in women's lives."

Female-focused social networking sites, like Urbanbaby.com and Clubmom.com, have grown dramatically and received media headlines of their own. In fact, millions of women and moms are marketed to online when just a few years ago that marketing was nonexistent.

Based on my professional experiences, it was around the same time that I started to notice my clients asking more about marketing to women. Clients who previously did not focus on women were starting to do so and those who had marketed to women wanted to do it more effectively. The advertising and public relations trade media also were starting to more deeply and frequently cover marketing-to-women topics.

"More and more companies are paying attention to women," McCann says. "Kellogg's, Procter & Gamble and Harley-Davidson seem to be doing good jobs of marketing to women. They believe in it and you see that commitment in action."

WALK IN WOMEN'S MANY SHOES

"Most marketers, though, have not caught up with their female consumers," stresses McCann. "Marketers are still not listening to women, both at the brand level and the agency level. I think agencies have a responsibility to keep clients informed. They need to care more about educating themselves and immersing themselves in women's lives. There is power in knowledge and the learning must be continuous. Life is not stagnant."

At Ketchum, the global public relations agency where I work, those same factors led to the development of a clear focus on the female consumer categorized as "Women 25 to 54." Later in the book, I will delve into the cornerstones of this approach and give some examples of how it plays out in the marketplace.

The theory underpinning the Women 25 to 54 approach was that women today are multi-minding. With all of the thoughts going on in her head, today's woman has little time for commercial messages. In fact, the seminal study on multi-minding, conducted by Ketchum Global Research in late 2005, indicated that, "Women 25 to 54 report that, on average, they think about 9.5 things in any given five-minute period." Furthermore, almost 6 in 10 women say they have much more on their minds now, compared with five years ago. That is 18 percent higher than the total public polled, 20 percent higher than men ages 25 to 54, and 35 percent higher than men in general.[1]

This prevalent, but as yet mostly unrecognized, phenomenon of multi-minding has major implications for any company seeking to speak to women buyers. First and foremost, women are less likely to say they have time for commercial messages. Women not only say they do not have time for commercial messages, but also report that they do not have time to devote undivided attention to consumer media. Women are much less likely than men to say that, on an average day, they frequently watch a television program from start to finish. In particular, 60 percent of men would say they frequently watch a full television program on an average day, while only 51 percent of women fall into this category. When it comes to listening to the radio for more than 30 minutes on an average day, 58 percent of men gave an affirmative response compared with 45 percent of women.[2]

In addition, women between the ages of 25 and 54 are less likely than all other groups surveyed—Americans, women, men, and men ages 25 to 54—to report that they frequently get to read a paper or magazine from start to finish, watch a television show from beginning to end, or listen to the radio for more than 30 minutes. More than half, or 59 percent, say they rarely or never read a newspaper from beginning to end, while 56 percent say they rarely or never read a magazine from cover to cover.[3]

More things are competing for women's attention, they are easily distracted, and they are not thinking just about themselves. Three-fourths agree that they spend more time thinking about the needs of others than their own. Women 25 to 54 are juggling numerous tasks and thoughts.[4]

SAME OLD ROUTINE NOT EFFECTIVE WITH WOMEN

It is no wonder, based on those statistics, that companies are starting to espouse "channel-neutral" marketing communications and not automatically defaulting to the traditional mediums of television, radio, and newspapers. In the marketing world, advertising via television, radio, and print has been the mainstay communications vehicle for decades. However, when you understand that the primary purchasers are multi-minding and not consuming traditional media, the channel-neutral approach makes a good deal of sense. Marketers should avoid a predetermination that advertising will be the primary method for marketing on television, in print, or through any other medium.

To effectively reach women, marketers should pick the channels that will work best and be open to all types of communication based on what will engage the consumer and address the challenges in the marketplace. You need to be where women are, not where you hope they are based on antiquated media buying models.

I knew more research was needed in the marketing-to-women space, but when we conducted and publicly launched the Women 25 to 54 research at Ketchum, even I was taken aback by the high level of interest from clients, prospects, and the media. *BusinessWeek* online, *BRANDWEEK* magazine, *CNNMoney*, the *Chicago Tribune*, *Fast Company*, and many others picked up on the multi-minding concept and related research.

With headlines like "Reaching Out to Today's Multi-Minding Woman" and "I Am Woman, Hear Me Shop," the media touted the concept. The media coverage drove even more interest from current and prospective clients. There has been more of a clamor for this type of information than I have ever seen in 20 years in the marketing communications business.

McCann notes that one of the biggest challenges in marketing to women is not in the external marketplace, but within the walls of companies.

"Change management is a big issue, still today," she says. "How do you get marketing-to-women efforts sold in to senior management is still a prevalent question with marketers."

That hot topic will be on the agendas at upcoming M2W Conferences so attendees can see the best-in-class initiatives and better understand how they can sell such concepts to their own companies.

"For those companies for whom marketing to women sounds too niche or gender-specific, start with an evolution of message," McCann advises. "The communication to women does not have to be blatant. Speak to what's important in her life—relationships, family, and an appreciation for her very busy life. Respect the totality of the consumer's life."

Marketers need to deal with this multi-minding mind-set, as well as the newly emerging competition. With the world waking up to the buying power of female consumers, many more marketers, both traditional and nontraditional, are competing for the limited mindshare of women. Clearly, a gap must be bridged.

KEYS TO THE FUTURE OF MARKETING TO WOMEN

I asked McCann what she thinks the future holds in terms of marketing to women and how marketers can bridge that gap. She has some intriguing predictions, ranging from the big picture to specific topics.

"Marketers need to show more concern for women's values," she notes. "That presents complications because values are across-the-board. Women are re-evaluating what they want out of life. Just a few years ago, women wanted it all. Today, they are making more quality choices. That's why you must constantly learn and engage in the marketplace."

McCann points out one of the common themes I heard from many of the experts interviewed for this book. Women today do not want it all. They want what is important to them and have a clear sense of priorities. They make purchasing decisions based on those priorities. More women are choosing family and children as their top priority. The Intelligence Group's Mom Intelligence Report calls it "x-treme" parenting and it is a macro-trend with moms, especially those in the X and Y generations—those 112 million people born between 1965 and 1992.[5] They have an intense devotion for mothering, with 91 percent of those included in the Mom Intelligence Report saying their greatest source of happiness comes from being a mother. The interview with Mimi Doe later in the book delves into this topic.

Another prediction from McCann is that "green" will continue to capture the attention of female consumers, although she thinks it will involve social responsibility rather than specific product attributes. "Our consumerism is over-the-top, ugly, and wanton. Women are re-evaluating how much they and their families need. I see a trend of being much less wasteful, and women are starting to actually be proud of their responsible behavior when it comes to less waste."

She believes parents are also reevaluating their kids' demands for "I want this" and "all my friends have it." Specifically, she thinks there will be a backlash with parents being proud of having less, not more, because it shows they are responsible.

Technology is another area that cannot be ignored, according to McCann. The key, much like with green, is using it responsibly.

"You can't go anywhere online without being accosted by marketing," she observes.

> There are great new avenues for online marketing, but how can marketers build profitable businesses without becoming pests? It's a real challenge. If marketers are a resource, not just marketing with commercial interests at heart, I think they can succeed in getting their messages across and still get business done.

McCann's predictions included one more trend that she thinks could supersede all others—the aging of the boomer generation:

> Talking to women as caregivers will be critically important and relevant for the group with more people than any other generation. As the population ages, women are the ones who feel the responsibility and take on the burdens—emotional and otherwise—of caring for their family, their employees, and themselves.
>
> This country is not yet prepared for the aging of this generation. And, Madison Avenue has rejected most topics that have to do with consumers and aging.… There seems to be a collective denial, but it will be one of the most important topics to women in the coming years.

Aging seems to be a reality that no one wants to talk about or address. We read daily about the shortages of nurses and nursing homes.

"There has not been a mass market tipping point in interest or action," McCann says. "Just like the marketing-to-women and marketing-to-moms areas, female consumers will lead the way. There will be a grassroots movement and then marketers will recognize the opportunity to market to the aging population."

JUST LISTEN TO THIS

When I asked McCann to tell me the one thing marketers should do when they market to women, she responded with one word, "listen."

"Marketers must listen to their female consumers and not enough are doing it. In all fairness, it's hard to do because listening implies that you will change what you are currently doing and some marketers have difficulty with that."

McCann realized the value of listening early in her career:

Once, when I was working at a company that wanted to target college-aged women in sororities, another woman and I were assigned to research their mindsets. I was an advocate for visiting them in their sorority houses, while my colleague thought we could understand them through quantitative data that we already had. My colleague could not believe her ears when she made the sorority visits. Their conversations were dominated by talk of marriage and they sang songs as groups, while the data showed they were career-oriented and individualistic. We would have missed valuable insights if we had just used the data.

Use all of your senses when marketing to women. Watch them. Listen to them. Taste what they are cooking. Be there, among them. It beats quantitative research hands down. Somewhere along the way, with all of the wonderful, sophisticated tools that are available to marketers, they forgot to use some of the most basic tools. Brands can be profitable and be forces for change. It's simple and complex at the same time.

With women becoming the apple of many marketers' eyes, there is more competition than ever to engage these powerful consumers. How will you successfully engage women? What about those predictions for the topics that will be important to women in the not-too-distant future? Nan McCann gave us some great insights.

We next hear from Marti Barletta, president of the TrendSight Group and author of several books, including the seminal book on marketing to women called *Marketing to Women: How to Understand, Reach, and Increase Your Share of the World's Largest Market Segment* (2003).

MARKETING NOT BOOMING WITH FEMALE BOOMERS

If the numbers are "huge" with women 25 to 54, the numbers are "unequivocal" and even more compelling with what Barletta calls

Questions Every Marketer or Business Owner Should Ask

- Do I know my audience from a qualitative and a quantitative perspective? Have I conducted research that enabled me to truly immerse myself in my audience's life, not just read about it?
- What mechanism for listening does my brand or business have? How am I changing my marketing based on that input? Am I communicating how I have changed back to the audience?
- What am I doing online to reach more women?
- Do I know the values of my female audience and am I responsive to those values?
- How does my brand or business provide a social responsibility benefit (green, sustainable, local) to my consumers?
- Is my brand or business prepared for an aging population and its needs? Am I actively cultivating relationships with women over age 50?

PrimeTime Women, those 50 to 70 years old. Barletta's 2007 book, *PrimeTime Women*, was the first book to examine the lucrative market of female consumers in that age group.

"It's the marketing trifecta, the intersection of a huge market in terms of numbers of people," explains Barletta. "It's where almost all of the population growth will happen in the next 10 years and it's the peak of lifetime salary range."

Astoundingly, "almost nothing" in terms of integrated, comprehensive, and consistent marketing is aimed at these women, according to Barletta. The prime-time segment seems to be where the mainstream marketing-to-women efforts were about a decade ago. The group is a powerful consumer force that has been virtually unrecognized by marketers in any meaningful way. Perhaps Barletta's book will do for marketing to prime-time women what her original book did for the topic of marketing to women generally—give it visibility and help marketers evolve their thinking and efforts.

Why and what can you do right now to attract these female consumers? Barletta notes that marketers make unfounded assumptions about prime-time consumers—namely, a cultural convention of being "youth-obsessed," a marketing fallacy that "if you get them while they are young, they are yours forever," and young marketers and agency staffers "cannot fathom that people in their 50s and 60s actually like their lives and are worth marketing to."

Actually, I see this phenomenon at work with marketing to women in a more general way. Many more male marketers and senior executives that I speak with still believe that marketing to women some-how results in ignoring men, youth, or some other audience. Certainly, there are some product categories or industries for which those audien-ces are the primary purchasers. Yet, women are routinely credited by research, major media, and marketing briefs as the primary purchasers 80 percent of the time. I would not be asking why you should market to women. I would be asking why you would not market to women.

BOOMING CONSUMER POWER

Barletta contends that prime-time women make an even higher per-centage of purchasing decisions than younger female consumers. Sev-eral important factors are driving that purchasing power. She explains:

> There are simply more single women in the 50- to 70-year-old group due to death (the expected lifespan of a woman is still longer than that of a man) or divorce, and they make 100 per-cent of their purchase decisions. For those who are still married, due to hormonal changes that make men less aggressive and women relatively more aggressive, and because in a long-lived relationship, the wife knows the husband's preferences well, she tends to lead or make the purchase decisions.

Just like female consumers below the age of 50, women in the prime-time group engage in multi-minding to manage the many dimen-sions of their life. I asked Barletta to speculate whether older women multi-mind to the same degree as younger women.

"At that age, women's roles as moms are typically not as consum-ing, the parts of the human brain that process information take more time and hearing may deteriorate, requiring more focus," she notes. "So, I would think that while multi-minding continues, it happens to a lesser degree with those in the 50- to 70-year-old range than with women aged 25 to 54."

UNMET NEEDS

If the multi-minding hurdle is lower, so to speak, what are the keys to reaching this lucrative audience? Barletta thinks it is very basic. "Don't ignore them," she implores.

That sounds so simple, right? Then, why is almost no one heeding the advice?

"No car company, no computer company, no bank, no financial services company has a consistent, comprehensive, integrated market-ing effort directed to women," notes Barletta, "even in cases where women are documented to be the primary customer."

A comprehensive campaign may not be aimed at prime-time women in particular, but individual pieces, like an ad or a Web site, are focused on this group. Even with the fragmented pieces, though, a key element seems to be missing … authenticity or really connecting with this woman in a relevant way.

Authenticity is "not a pink campaign or packaging," Barletta notes.

> And it's probably easier to achieve with a female audience than a male audience. Men tend to be hierarchical and aspirational, whereas women tend to be more accepting of the "real you." They are more comfortable with who they are. Marketing that reflects who they really are, not who they aspire to be, will be far more authentic to them.

It is important to note that while authenticity has become a favorite buzzword in the marketing world, I do not think it is just a passing trend—especially with female consumers of all ages. Authenticity and all of its implications, such as credibility, transparency, relevance, consumer-centeredness, and corporate social responsibility, will continue to permeate consumer minds and their decision making.

M^2 Must-Dos

- ✓ Use a variety of channels and espouse more of a channel-neutral approach to market to women.
- ✓ Immerse yourself in the marketplace and really "walk in her shoes" to understand important nuances of your female audience.
- ✓ Listen to real women in your target audience and make changes based on their input.
- ✓ Do not ignore prime-time women.

Chapter Three

What's Wrong? Why Current Marketing Efforts Are Not Working

Stacy DeBroff, chief executive officer and founder of Mom Central Consulting in Chestnut Hill, Massachusetts, notes that advertisements feature—

> manly men who can help us clean better, like Mr. Clean and the Brawny man, or female nymphs, like the woman sprawled on a mountaintop on an Evian bottle or the woman wearing only ribbons in an ad for Olay ... think for a moment just about the images used by marketers....
>
> I am not a bald man, a brawny man, or a nymph. I wear more than ribbons and I bet most other women do, too. There is clearly a mismatch between brand images and their female consumers.

Almost universally, the thought-leaders, chief marketing officers, book authors, social networking experts, and women with whom I talk believe that marketing to women and marketing to moms are areas that have finally been recognized by marketers as real and lucrative. Therefore, it is no surprise that marketers and businesses have put more time and effort into those areas.

MOMS: THE NEW SUPER-CONSUMERS

Headlines and research about the buying power of women, and especially of moms, are rampant. *USA Today* proclaims, "Alpha Moms Leap to Top of Trendsetters" and notes, "She ignites markets."[1] The Intelligence Group's Mom Intelligence Report concludes, "Moms are perhaps the most important consumer group in the United States, and they are the primary purchaser for nearly every consumer goods category, spending $1.7 trillion a year, as well as increasingly influencing other household purchases, such as automobiles and financial services."[2]

An *Advertising Age* magazine article, entitled "Mommy Blogs: A Marketer's Dream," shares why a growing number of well-produced sites can put marketers in touch with an affluent and loyal audience of moms online.[3] *Editor & Publisher* magazine asks "What Do Women Want?" in its article about trying to attract women back to reading newspapers, because women "have never been more attractive to advertisers."[4]

Despite the new level of attention, marketers do not find that their efforts are working as well as they would like. If you listen to DeBroff, you will learn a great deal about why this is the case. This chapter explores the steps marketers can take to overcome current challenges and really start to resonate with women, particularly those who are also moms.

TOO BUSY FOR COMMERCIAL MESSAGES

Today's female consumer is busy and has a complex web of duties that makes her less than readily available to most marketers. Research has shown that while about half of the total public, men, and men 25 to 54 agree that they have little time for commercial messages, women are even more likely to feel a time crunch. Sixty-one percent of women in general and 62 percent of women 25 to 54 say they have little time for such messages. The challenge is exacerbated with moms, 65 percent of whom say they have little time for commercial messages.[5]

There is definitely a time-crunch issue, mostly driven by the female consumers themselves. Yet, there are other reasons why current marketing is not working that rest more on the shoulders of marketers and businesses. More and more research and an increasing number of articles, especially in the trade press, show that current marketing is not meeting the needs of today's female consumers.

"Newspapers are losing working mothers and time-pressed single women even faster than they are losing readers overall," notes a recent article from *Editor & Publisher*. "This loss is happening at exactly the time (when) working mothers and busy singles have never been more attractive to advertisers."[6]

COSTLY MISTAKES

In their book, *Trillion Dollar Mom$*, Bonnie Ulman and Maria Bailey (2005) talk extensively about how companies currently promoting their products to mothers are falling short in understanding how the mom market is changing. Moms represent $1.7 trillion in buying power, yet they give marketers a failing grade in marketing to them. According to *Trillion Dollar Mom$*, only 20 percent of mothers said advertisers were doing a good job connecting with them, while 70 percent said marketers are not focused on moms in their advertising. Thirty percent said they see ads that offend them.

What is going on?

Much of the coverage that speculates about why current marketing is not working suggests areas of common mistakes. Believing that "focusing on women will alienate men," and that "female consumer marketing requires less funding," are two of the costliest mistakes, according to Andrea Learned, author of *Don't Think Pink.*[7]

Based on the discussions I have had and the research I have seen over the past few years, marketing to women boils down much like the old "three Rs" adage of long ago. Instead of "reading," "'riting" (writing), and "'rithmetic" (arithmetic), the three Rs now apply to relevance, reality, and relationships. Like many things in this book, this approach sounds deceptively simple, but are you following it? Probably not.

Well, let us look at a subcategory of women that is one of the most important consumer groups in the United States—moms. In almost every consumer-goods category, moms serve as the chief purchasing officer for the household.

SMART SOLUTIONS

To explore the reasons why current marketing efforts are not working, I discussed the issue with DeBroff. In addition to being president and founder of Mom Central, a consulting firm focused on "smart solutions for busy moms," she is a television and radio personality, bestselling author, and parenting guru. As a regular guest on the *Today* show, she is often asked about how companies can connect with today's time-pressed moms. She is quick witted, has a great sense of humor, and has great insights, as well as plenty of examples, to share.

"Mothers today are really smart. They went to school, worked for a while or still do, and wanted to be astronauts, senators, and really good mothers," DeBroff explains. "I did not aspire to be a toilet paper roll changer, and I am not a joyful floor mopper. I can't identify with those images and resent marketing that makes me and other moms seem like we should happily embrace those roles."

Indeed, what it means to be a mom has changed since past generations. Today, 72 percent of moms also work outside the home.[8] There are myriad ways to combine motherhood and working outside of the home—and just as many Web sites, blogs, and social networking sites to help. One of the sites I like best is Mommytrackd.com, the "working mother's guide to managed chaos."

The site is in tune with women who have children, but speaks to them as women rather than just talking to them as moms. The site keenly and consistently uses the filter of "busy women with no time" and provides quick information and useful tips that cater to both the woman and the mom dimensions. Most sites like Mommytrackd.com have been around for only a few years, although the struggles of managing home and work life have existed for decades.

MADISON AVENUE TOO REMOVED FROM MOST MOMS

Amy Keroes, founder and chief executive officer of mommytrackd.com, believes that "the reason Madison Avenue is having difficulty reaching busy women is that these women are not consuming traditional media the way they used to, the use of TIVO has reduced the effectiveness of television advertising, and women have transferred their attention to the Web."

Just as cable network options exploded and suddenly we had access to hundreds of channels, online offerings are now expanding rapidly. Women will find the sites where they feel comfortable, particularly sites that filter the noise and the marketing and use a voice that resonates with them.

Keroes observes—

Thirty- and 60-second advertising spots that speak to everyone are a thing of the past. But just like marketers knew that women who read *Allure Magazine* are apt to read *InStyle Magazine*, smart marketers today can amass significant reach and micro-target at the same time by engaging 'families of sites' that have similar content."

I believe sites like Mommytrackd.com will be the shopping malls of the future—shortcuts that women take to quickly find what they like in the amount of time they have to spare.

"If they like the filter of content that a site provides, women will probably like the product picks as well," says Keroes. "Our audience wants good content, so we work hard to help marketers on our site get their message right. Even if a marketer provides 'sponsored content,' as long as we are honest about the purpose, women on the site seem to embrace it."

Clearly, mommytrackd is in tune with its target audience, but not all marketers are as effective.

"Brand and brand managers are not intrinsically in tune with the mom market and many marketers are so used to traditional ways," says DeBroff. "The days of a public address system for communicating with a single tagline, banner ads, and generalized information are gone.

Moms are so busy that they want to solve very specific problems and want personalized feedback. They are discerning and do not want to be manipulated."

That is a tall order to fill, especially when marketers and businesses think about the strategic and cost implications associated with moving away from mass approaches toward those that are perceived to be more specific, personalized, and certainly less manipulative. "Is it possible to achieve all this?" DeBroff insists it is.

MULTI-MINDING MOM MESSAGING

"What you need to do as a marketer all comes down to elevating a message that captures moms across all variations of who mom is today," DeBroff explains.

> You need to build messages around a core need or anxiety that will be relevant to a mom. Eating as a family, nutritious meals, health, and education are core needs and high sources of anxiety for most moms. If your brand can honestly help to solve one of those challenges, even in a small way, that's a golden message.

> It is really a combination of message elevation and message relevance—which I call message relevation—that is the sweet spot. Imagine if your brand or business could craft its messages in such a way that elevates the message to address a core need that, in turn, makes the brand more relevant to consumers' lives. Perhaps you are thinking this holy grail of messaging is reserved for a certain tier of products and services.

Can any one brand or business rise to the challenge of message relevation? Absolutely, says DeBroff.

> Take a common product like toilet paper. No mom likes toilet paper because no one in the household changes toilet paper rolls but mom. But when Cottonelle invented toilet paper with a picture of a puppy on every fifth sheet, it enabled kids to use just enough, but not too much, toilet paper. That simple product innovation and the associated messages showed us that Cottonelle was making our toilet paper-changing job, which we resent, just a bit easier. We like that.
>
> Another great example is Swiffer. We all want clean floors, but we hate every moment we have to spend cleaning them. Swiffer can help us clean our floors in 30 seconds. We can be June Cleaver and a modern woman at the same time. It's gratifying.

Surely, if companies that make toilet paper and floor mops can tweak their products and "relevate" their messages, then any company can. But why, then, is it so uncommon? It goes back to being deceptively simple. It seems simple, but the thinking is really quite ingenious and stems from being in tune with the mom audience.

So how might the "relevation" concept apply to a higher-end, more complex product? Consider laundry machines. Doing the laundry is certainly a mundane task, but washers and dryers have become high-tech. DeBroff says,

> No mom likes to do laundry and we certainly don't trust those who say they do. It's the bane of our existence, but if a company that sells washers and dryers tells me I can double the amount of laundry per load and that their machines won't break down, I care about those things.

Yes, even companies that make laundry appliances can "relevate" their messages.

Next, let's consider another common product that can be associated with expensive service, the cell phone.

"It's not the functionality or the family and friends plan. They are ubiquitous," DeBroff surmises. "Protecting our kids and no surprises with costs are the core needs that drive moms in this category. If you can convince moms your cell phone is able to deliver on safety and she won't get a $250 bill for text messages … sold."

Clearly, the relevance of the messaging and the reality of the images are major contributors to showing moms that your brand or business understands them. Based on research and the reactions of thought-leaders in the marketing-to-moms space, there is much work to be done in the areas of relevance and reality.

RELATIONSHIPS: THE ROOT OF SUCCESS

In addition to relevance and reality, relationships—yes, real relationships—with female consumers are a critical success factor in future marketing efforts. Numerous studies are pointing to "family and friends" now being the most credible sources of information for women who are considering a purchase decision. That means women are relying on the opinions of other women in their local communities and their online communities as the most trusted sources for recommendations and referrals.

"Marketing has not been about relationship building and moms today are skeptical," says DeBroff.

> Brands need to enter the river of trusted information, which is formed by the opinions of trusted family and friends. Your

relationships with consumers enable your brand to become a floating canoe on that river. Once you build that trust, there is a predisposition to listen. Women are now listening to Dove and what the brand will do next because of the positive impact of its Real Beauty campaign, which focused on a core area of anxiety for mothers—girls' self-esteem.

A number of the thought-leaders I have talked with espouse this same belief—real relationships between brands or businesses and their consumers will be nonnegotiable for success in the future. This approach is almost completely opposite of what traditionally has been done in marketing with mass approaches, especially for national brands or services. The Internet is enabling much more one-on-one marketing than was ever done in the past. An Internet marketing effort, however, does not equal an effective relationship-building approach in and of itself.

To build relationships, DeBroff advocates using "the unfiltered voices of real moms, brand evangelists who are bloggers and authors, talking with real moms versus just the use of quantitative studies, and really being in synch with the brains of your moms."

"We've been able to find a voice that our readers like and want," adds Keroes. "Once women find a site they trust, they pay attention to the marketing wrapped in that voice."

DeBroff cites a number of examples where the voices of real moms have propelled businesses into that "river of trust" without much other marketing. She notes,

Whole Foods can get moms to spend twice as much as they might usually because we trust them to read labels for us. Whole Foods enables moms to save time and have choices around the high-anxiety area of nutritional meals.

Moms also love Costco, which enables us to buy a 36-roll package of toilet paper, so we don't have to buy it for a while, and Trader Joe's for a great combination of high-quality ingredients at a low price. These brands have tremendous word-of-mouth value among moms.

These companies have built fairly trusted relationships with their consumers based on core needs of those consumers. Interestingly, these marketers have let go of their message and entrusted their consumers to carry it for them. It seems risky, but in the future, not letting go will be the bigger risk. Not letting go will be seen as unauthentic and less credible.

DeBroff believes that the credibility generated by the voices of real moms could be applied to categories and industries that have not yet employed the approach. She pointed out that the pharmaceutical industry spends huge amounts of money for customer acquisition.

"If those companies could ride the viral wave of moms who just love their products because the products have truly helped someone they know, the cost for patient acquisition would decrease significantly," she believes.

BRANDS WILL LIVE IN THE HANDS OF MOMS

Just the other day, I read an article in the big marketing trade magazine, *BRANDWEEK.* The headline said, "Lose Control: It's Good for Your Brand."[9] The article explains that losing control does not mean losing control of your brand or your message. It does mean that most brands have a fan base that can and should be trusted. It takes time for those relationships to be built through involvement, rather than through just a mass message. More on how brands will be co-managed by consumers will be explored in chapter 14.

Just as relationships in real life take time to build, so, too, does it take time and effort to build a trusting relationship with consumers. Brand managers, who are assigned to a brand for 12 to 18 months, do not appear to have a vested stake in the long-term success of their brand. In that case, relationship-building can be institutionalized through communications agencies (advertising and public relations, usually) that stay with a brand longer than the average brand manager. The agencies should be immersed personally in the female consumer audience and not just reading research.

Consistent online efforts, local marketing events, consumer panels, key blogger relationships, partnerships with social networking sites, and other vehicles that enable you to forge a real relationship with your female consumers are crucial.

According to a recent Intelligence Group's Mom Intelligence Report, "Regardless of the stage of motherhood they are in, women are flocking to online social networks."[10] DeBroff predicts social networking sites will become a standard practice in marketing to women and moms.

"It won't just be one site. Moms gather information from a variety of online sites," says DeBroff. "There will be some central gathering sites, but others will change and you'll need to adapt—another reason to really be in synch with moms."

DeBroff's prediction is already becoming reality as Facebook introduced a service called Beacon, which allows its member who opt-in to send a note to their profile pages when they buy something from an online site. Facebook friends will know when and what was purchased, in effect, effortlessly sharing a recommendation. When I predicted at the beginning of this book that traffic to branded Web sites would slow, it was because of this type of activity.

Questions Every Marketer or Business Owner Should Ask

- Do I know if my marketing is connecting with women and moms?
- What percentage of my female audience would say my brand or business does not understand them?
- What core anxiety or issue does my brand or business address, and how can I "relevate" my message to reflect it?
- Do I and do others in my organization have real, one-on-one relationships with women in our core audience, and are we getting input from them?
- Are the images we use to communicate our brand or business in synch with the reality of our female audience?

Social networking sites, enabling users to automatically make recommendations and endorsements through purchase confirmations, will become that "river of trusted information" that DeBroff described. Branded community sites do not have enough bonding material for female consumers.

Both DeBroff and Keroes agree that you need to be a repeat player to form relationships. Current efforts are not working in part because it takes more time than the life of one campaign or the tenure of a brand manager to forge relationships. Engaging trusted sources—both online and offline—to elevate your message and serve as brand ambassadors can accelerate that critical relationship-building.

As keys to cementing relationships with women, DeBroff and Keroes recommend "getting in synch with moms' brains" and ensuring that you "don't condescend to the modern woman." It certainly makes me wonder about the logic behind those images of men on cleaning products who can show the "little woman" how to clean.

Leslie Morgan Steiner, author of the *Mommy Wars* (2006), offers a perspective that I think sums up the issue perfectly. She says,

Based on my experience—talking to hundreds of moms in writing *Mommy Wars*, and listening to 100,000-plus comments posted on my On Balance "mommyblog"—the biggest mistake marketers make is when they use stereotyped ideals of perfect moms that end up making real mothers feel like bad mothers. Working mom, stay-at-home mom, pre-mom, alpha mom, mocha mom, stepmom, slacker mom, Mr. Mom—we are all completely unprepared for the immense job of loving our kids and juggling our lives. We try, every minute of every day, to be the best parent, employee, spouse, and friend we can. An enormous opportunity exists for marketers to encourage moms to rejoice in our individuality and to feel good about ourselves. Products and messages that celebrate motherhood, instead of subtly or not-so-subtly chiding us for falling short of an unrealistic cultural stereotype, engender lasting, long-term loyalty from women everywhere.

Amen to that.

M^2 Must-Dos

✓ Match your brand or business image with those of your female consumers.
✓ Structure your brand or business communications for relevance, reality, and relationship-building.
✓ "Relevate" your message to match a core need or anxiety of your audience.
✓ Engage trusted sources as filters for your brand or business.
✓ Do not condescend to women, either in images or by ignoring what it really is like to be in their shoes.
✓ Cater to the female side of a mom by replacing downtime with pleasant surprises or indulgences, like offering hand massages while she waits in a salon for a haircut.

Chapter Four

Why Are We So Hard to Reach? The Challenge of Marketing to Women 25 to 54

"Each day is an exercise in choreography," explains Susan, a mother of two-year-old twins, about her life as a working mom. Because she and her husband Rick both have jobs, they have been compelled to incorporate much more flexibility into their daily schedules since the birth of the twins. Full-time, in-home child care is a necessity to bridge the dual work schedules.

Fortunately, they both like to cook, although Susan does the grocery shopping, meal planning, and most of the food preparation. Since the children are not yet in school, the social calendars for Susan, Rick and the children are limited primarily to shopping, play dates with the neighbor's children, and get-togethers with friends.

"I feel like there's so much on the agenda and not enough time to go around now," says Susan. "What will happen to our schedules when we add school and social activities to the mix?"

MULTI-MINDING IS PERVASIVE

Women like Susan are constantly juggling a mix of career, family, and self-care decisions at any given moment—multi-minding. All of their multi-tasking and multi-minding efforts leave less time for commercial messages to seep in. Every time I explain the multi-minding concept to women, without fail, they say, "That's me!" Just recently, I spoke with a woman who is a mom and has a high-profile political job. When I explained the concept of multi-minding, she said, "Consider me Exhibit A. That's my life exactly."

Research conducted by the Ketchum Global Research Network shows that 58 percent of women ranging in age from 25 to 54 have much more on their minds today than they did just five years ago. Not only do women have more on their minds, but they have much more on their minds compared with men and the general public.

We know they have a lot on their minds, but let's dig into just what is competing for your female customers' attention. First, consider the staggering number of media outlets, consumer magazines, radio stations, and online sites that inundate American homes every day. Just counting the media, we have hundreds of television networks, thousands of consumer magazines, tens of thousands of radio stations, tens of millions (and growing by the minute) of Web sites, and hundreds of millions of blogs. I have seen estimates of the number of commercial messages that the average person is exposed to on a daily basis that range from 250 to 5,000, depending on the study. Even at the conservative end, the numbers are large and growing.

In addition to the barrage of media, women's busy lifestyles create even more challenges and make it more difficult for marketers to reach them. Multi-tasking continues to be a prevalent method for managing daily activities as women report living the "Thirty-Eight Hour Day" by packing 38 hours of activity into a 24-hour period.[1]

Given that women are trying to pack 38 hours of activity into a 24-hour period and barely have enough time to meet their personal needs, how and when will you ever get through to them? With all of this "busy-ness," how can a marketer successfully reach multi-minding women? As with many things, it all starts at home.

START AT HOME TO REACH MULTI-MINDERS

Home is where the heart is. Believe it or not, it is also where the success of your business will be decided. It is the place where women are most often gathering information and opinions, and it is a place that can unlock the secrets of how to reach them.

Sitting and talking with women in a relaxed atmosphere, not in a formal focus group, reveals deep and telling details of how their lives are changing. Such casual conversations are effective in understanding the major dimensions of women's lives, like what they care about most, and in drawing out critical implications for marketers. I call them "homecomings."

These "homecoming" conversations are so valuable that even A. G. Lafley, chief executive officer of the consumer products powerhouse Procter & Gamble, makes time in his day to sit and talk with real women in their homes. He calls it "mother-in-law research" and he uses it to maintain a direct line to the consumer. Not only does Lafley spend time in consumers' homes, but he also expects his senior leadership to do the same.

"It is all about staying really close to the consumer, identifying exactly what she wants, and providing just that," Lafley notes.[2]

The technique seems smart—and it is. However, it is a not-so-secret weapon that thought-leaders in the marketing-to-women space have been engaging for years—talking to women in their homes about things that matter to them. Ask and they will tell you, *if* you have a genuine interest in making their lives and the lives of their families better in some way.

In my experiences, though, many professional communicators, brand managers, and business owners are still sitting in their offices looking at page after page of qualitative research reports that attempt to tell them what female consumers want. Facts and data are needed and certainly help companies make informed business decisions. When marketing to women who have so many things on their minds, however, facts and data are just not enough. The passion and sincerity that come through loud and clear in person may never be evident with a representative sample or an Internet survey.

Another popular technique, especially in established businesses, is what I call the "I asked my wife" technique. That technique is used whenever a senior, often older, male executive asks his wife what she thinks about how his company is marketing a certain product, such as skin care lotion or baby food. It is great to get women talking, but their response may be invalid if that particular woman does not color her own hair or have small children—and neither do her friends. Therefore, be careful that the women you consult and listen to match the women who actually buy your product.

After a number of these discussions, trends will emerge and what women are saying will certainly change how we will do business in the future. Conduct "homecomings" for your business in neighborhoods or key markets where high concentrations of women currently are buying your product or service. Listen to what they are saying, identify common trends, use those themes to create your messages, and court them to be ambassadors for your brand.

Mimi Doe, parenting guru, Oprah guest, and author of *Busy but Balanced* (2001) and other books, inspires tens of thousands of women with her insightful tips, seminars and newsletters. What is the secret to her ability to inspire, motivate, and identify marketplace trends? She talks with and listens to women—often in their homes, but also online, in line at the local grocery store, and anytime she can.

"Literally sit in *their* circle," advocates Doe. These conversations give her powerful insights and a keen ability to identify future trends. In her award-winning book, *Busy but Balanced*, Doe in many ways predicted the trend of "multi-minding" based on her many consumer connections. She heard and saw that women were struggling with managing busy work schedules, cooking healthy meals, attending kids' baseball practices and piano lessons, staying in touch with friends, doing the grocery shopping, and washing the mountain of laundry.

At the same time, these women sought harmony and balance in their lives. Hence, the premise of *Busy but Balanced* was born, and the concept is even more relevant today than it was just a few years ago.

Doe has counseled thousands of women on how to restore order to the chaos that is often a hallmark of their busy lives.

I was intrigued to get Doe's perspective on how marketers can successfully interject marketing messages into the incredibly action-packed lives of women today. As I expected, she has great advice.

"Talking directly with women should be at the top of your list," Doe offers. Here are some other enlightening perspectives and ideas that have surfaced in her many conversations with women.

PRIORITIES TRUMP BALANCE

Let's revisit the concept of "busy-ness." Indeed, women today are busier than ever, but Doe recently uncovered a growing nuance to this busy life, and it will certainly affect how we communicate with multi-minding women.

Marketers must know that moms—the highly sought-after female consumer type and the focus of Doe's work—are choosing quality of life over balancing it all.

"This evolving attitude will drive different purchases and will most certainly drive a change in how we market those products and services," predicts Doe.

"Balance" has been such a hot-button word for women, particularly when referring to how to "do it all" and do it all gracefully. Well, just as multi-tasking has been replaced by multi-minding, balance is on its way out, too. Balance is passé, you say? That is exactly what Doe's research is showing.

She is convinced that balance is being phased out by prioritization. Rather than balancing it all, moms are actively pursuing ways to honor what has become a driving priority—time with their children, especially when those children are young.

Interestingly, the groups of moms who are driving this trend—Gen Xers and Gen Yers (or the Millennials)—were brought up by working mothers who had less flexibility in the workplace and, therefore, needed other avenues, like day care, to help with the children. They are now saying they want to be more available to their kids than their mothers were to them, and in many ways, are returning to a more traditional lifestyle experienced when moms did not work as much.

TRADITION WITH A TWIST

Yet, this phenomenon is not just a pure return to tradition because there are major twists, as Doe notes.

"These moms are educated. They likely worked full time before having children and are making very deliberate choices to work less, or work differently, in order to spend time with their children," she says. "What's more, they are encouraging their spouses to do the same."

Just like Susan and Rick, they are creating a tag-team approach that ideally enables both parents to spend more time with their children. Less work often means less income, but if the priority is time with their children, it is a trade-off more and more parents are willing to make.

Less income means less purchasing power, which spells bad news for marketers. Right? Not exactly. This educated, experienced woman who is primarily in charge of her family's spending is going to be the most discerning consumer yet, according to Doe. "Mindful" is a good word to describe her. She is proud of her choices, in control of her spending, and not worried about what others think.

She will buy a less-expensive home to enable herself and her spouse to work less. She will look for high quality at a reasonable price. Superfluous purchases go out the window of the expensive house.

"One really helpful magazine will replace the subscriptions to five magazines and that one will be passed along to her sister," Doe predicts.

In addition, products that serve a variety of functions will replace niche products. Parents will find more time to spend with their families by using products that are healthy and multifunctional. As a result, these multifunctional products will be in demand. Bye-bye to the bathroom cleaner, kitchen counter wipes, and window sprays. Hello to the multisurface, nontoxic, nice-smelling, works-in-all-rooms cleaner.

"Once this mindful, choosy consumer latches on to something she is happy with, she will become an evangelist and practically sell the product for you," says Doe.

WOMEN CAN SMELL A RAT

How do you, as a local business or a megabrand, reach this discerning female consumer who is looking for quality and multifunctionality that enable her to spend more time with her family and to create a healthy and happy environment? One of the most important ways to reach this consumer is through credible, *authentic* communications. Doe stresses that authenticity is a key to reaching women, especially moms.

But what is authentic to these women? Think back to Susan. There are groups she belongs to and places she goes because they involve her priorities in life—her children, her health, her friends, and her work. If you can reach her through those channels, your messages will be more credible. And if those messages are then delivered in that credible venue by a messenger she trusts, such as a family member or friend, or in a local setting, they can reach true authenticity.

For instance, Susan belongs to a local "Mothers of Multiples" group. When another mom of multiples, Jan, comes to the group and says she is having problems with her current baby wipes—they leave lint on the baby and everything else she wipes with them—and is asking for the advice of other moms, the responses come pouring in. Specific brands are referenced and recommended. Uses for baby wipes, ranging from wiping the baby's bottom to dusting furniture, wiping the hands and faces of toddlers, and removing lint from skirts, flow through the conversation thread. The next baby wipes purchasing decision being considered by Susan, Jan, and thousands of other mothers is now being aired and made via this online forum. These women buy a lot of baby wipes and other products, and the decisions they make are being heavily influenced by other mothers.

REACH WOMEN WHERE THEY ARE

Three things are happening here that you can employ: local venues, credible messages, and authentic messengers.

Reach women where they are and remember they are not "national" beings. They live in a particular town, city, or market. Conduct "homecomings" on local levels and use those findings to target the local media. Talk and dig deep. Get at the emotion, not just the facts. You will see trends emerge. Then, wrap up the local findings to identify trends and create a national plan.

Many of the companies with which I have worked have not yet taken that approach. Instead, they continue to create national campaigns with the hopes they will trickle down to the local level. Credibility is built from the ground up, not from the top down. In the political arena, it is called micro-targeting and it is working to sway and win female voters. More on that in chapter 10.

Focus your messages on one thing that really resonates with your particular female consumer. Keep the messages clean and simple and make them believable.

"Women, and especially moms, have a keen ability to smell a rat," observes Doe.

If you are selling skin care products that make skin look more youthful and reduce fine lines, do not forget to tell her that she has to use each of the six products every day for two months before she will see results. If she knows the whole truth going in, you will have met her expectations. If she feels deceived, you will have lost her—and her sister, her mother, her three closest friends, the 10 women in the local Mothers of Preschoolers group, and the 20 women a day who visit her blog. Talk about a negative return on investment.

Doe knows that moms want advice from other moms. Local Meetup. com group organizers or leaders of local moms' or women's groups are exceptionally credible messengers when they believe in something. These local leaders can serve as point people, influencers, and

---

Questions Every Marketer or Business Owner Should Ask

- Am I visiting with my consumers in their homes?
- Do I have information from and about my consumers from qualitative, not just quantitative, sources?
- Have we involved the target audience of women in creating and disseminating our messages?
- Have we identified the most credible messengers to deliver our messages?
- Am I helping my female consumers to shape the world the way *they* want it?

---

evangelists for your brand. The challenge is that these messengers cannot be paid. If they are, they are much less credible.

In fact, these women would likely feel uncomfortable taking payment because their opinions would no longer be authentic. There is something they want, however, that you can give them—that is, content with real, credible, authentic information and tips, along with experiences, and easy purchasing options that save them time.

Busy women and moms welcome the quick, simple, healthy dinner recipes like those e-mailed weekly by Mealtime.org; one-click online shopping provided by Amazon.com; and in-home, personalized clothes shopping like the women's clothing site Etcetera.com.

Overall, the transparency that is being demanded by Wall Street and investors of public business is also being demanded increasingly by female consumers. Discerning and intelligent female consumers want simple choices that multi-task. Doe believes they want to be more involved than ever in their choices, so give them a reason to be invested. They want you to understand their world and to speak to them where they live.

"They are thoughtful, mindful, and fully capable of shaping the world around them that *they* want, not what the world around them wants to give them," adds Doe.

PRIORITIES, NOT TRADITIONAL WORK SCHEDULES, WILL SHAPE THE FUTURE

Expect future generations of women to accelerate those trends. The children of these women will be exposed to many new ways to work and will support key priorities like time with children. Doe further predicts that scouring flea markets, with kids in tow, to find antique brooches to sell on eBay may be just as common as a mom working in a city office for an accounting firm. Work choices may net fewer dollars in favor of time, and product preferences and purchases will change with these trends.

So, if you are trying to figure out how you will get into the minds of your female consumers as they try to pack 38 hours of activity into their 24-hour day, start at home. The home holds the keys to her mind and her heart.

M^2 Must-Dos

✓ Communicate in local venues.
✓ Identify credible messages.
✓ Engage authentic messengers.
✓ Engage women who believe in your product as brand ambassadors.
✓ Provide content to local moms' groups that can be used and shared.
✓ Conduct local "homecoming" conversations as the basis for your local or national campaign. These local conversations should "trickle-up."

Chapter Five

Remaking the Clock: Women and the 38-Hour Day

Without pausing, Patty says,

> I really want to be able to feed my family three nutritious meals
> a day, talk for more than 30 seconds with my husband, check
> off all of my 'to-dos' at work, prepare for that big meeting
> tomorrow, help with homework, attend the school concert,
> climb the mountain of laundry, give back in some way to the
> community, find a few minutes to read or just decompress, and
> maybe get to the bathroom, but all of that takes more time than
> any human has in a day.

Notice that she did not say she wanted, nor does she have time for, things
she considers to be extraneous, like listening to or watching commercial
messages.

According to several studies, women actually do pack 38 hours of
activity into a 24-hour day on a regular basis. "I don't know how she
does it" is a commonly used phrase and is even the title of a recently
published book, referring to how women do all they have to do. Consumers are doing more than 24 hours worth of activities in one day,
which can easily lead to the assumption that any one activity receiving
undivided attention is becoming more unlikely. In fact, research shows
that 62 percent of busy, multi-minding women like Patty say they have
little or no time for commercial messages.[1]

Where does that leave marketers? Well, marketers need to rethink
their ideas about a 24-hour day and find an appropriate place for their
messages. It is not an easy challenge, but it is certainly one that must be
addressed, especially if female consumers are important to your business.

Women are, indeed, master jugglers. Research shows they are often
overstressed, are overworked, and have precious little time for

themselves. Many activities compete for their attention and they feel pulled in many directions. I cannot recall a recent conversation with any woman when at least one of the topics was not how she was going to do all she had to do that day or that week.

In a poll that I conducted on my own blog, Toobusytoshop.blogspot. com, the response was unanimous. Every woman who participated, when asked to cast a vote on the degree of her multi-minding, said "constantly."

In her book, *Hannah Keeley's Total Mom Makeover* (2007), Hannah Keeley, founder of Totalmom.com and the mother of seven children, addresses how moms specifically can pack more activities into their day by "piggybacking tasks." This piggybacking is a great, real-life example of multi-tasking and multi-minding at work.

Keeley says,

> We have to develop our minds to see little pockets of opportu-
> nity and take full advantage of them. When we take a minute to
> use the bathroom, we can wipe off the counter after we wash
> our hands. When we walk through the living room, we can pick
> up four toys on our way. We can take multi-tasking to an
> entirely new level, making it more like an art than a coping
> mechanism. You can easily double or triple your accomplish-
> ments when you learn how to piggyback your tasks.[2]

Whether she is a work-outside-the-home woman or a mom who is an at-home manager, time is at a premium and our female consumers are clearly busy. The Internet and its wealth of information certainly have helped multi-minding women remake their day. Around-the-clock access to anything and anyone enables women to be productive at any time of the day or night. They love avoiding holiday traffic and crowded malls by being able to shop online at midnight. They can save time by having groceries delivered to their doorstep. If Patty forgets to send a birthday gift to her brother in Florida, needs to find new school uniforms, wants to look up medical information, or has to pay bills at 3 A.M., she can accomplish all of these tasks with fast, abundant help at her fingertips.

This access to information, tips, shopping, reviews, and much, much more has actually accelerated women's ability to multi-task and multi-mind. As a result, thanks to the decrease in time that it takes to get things done online, they can now fit more activities into a given day.

It makes sense, therefore, that many marketers are trying to inter-cept consumers online, where they often spend an enormous amount of time surfing the Internet. According to *BRANDWEEK* magazine, "The Internet is a major gathering place for today's women, and savvy marketers are tapping its power to provide information, and create community and conversations about brands."[3]

While mass numbers of women are online due to the millions of Web sites and blogs, each with its own micro-audience, it can be a challenge to actually reach those masses. Huge numbers of consumers can be reached online through search engines, which serve as the gateway to the time efficiency that women crave. In fact, a number of studies are now showing that search engines and the power of search are primary keys in reaching consumers today. The power of search resides not in the banner ads, but in the placement of your site in the search results and how your site is linked to others, both of which imply usage and credibility.

According to ComScore, an Internet marketing research company, food product sites drew 93.7 million visitors collectively during the three-month study period, with 47 percent of these visitors being directed to the site from a search engine. Baby care sites got an even bigger proportion of these visitors, or 60 percent of the 26 million unique visitors, from a search.[4] These audience numbers are bigger than the majority of audiences for television or print media buys for most packaged-goods companies.

Moms, sisters, and best girlfriends used to be the first places a woman would turn for advice on just about anything from recipes to recommendations on raising children. In some ways, real-life family and friends have been replaced by search engines as the primary portals for seeking advice. In my experiences, women with and without children are using search tools, such as Google and Yahoo!, as the *first* resource of choice when looking for information or advice. The ability to conduct an online search has emerged as one of the fastest ways for consumers to get the information they want, literally helping women put more time into their day.

While many women spend a great deal of time online, they still lead real, offline lives, as well. Remaking the day to include commercial messages may be even more difficult in real life than it is online. Getting women to participate in an event means they must see enough value in it to make it a destination and likely give up doing something else. You gain strong commitment through this type of involvement, but it is difficult to achieve significant participation.

One smart way to gain offline attention is to connect your product or brand with an event or organization where women are already gathering. A tip in a previous chapter suggested that you can succeed by enabling a woman's time to do double or triple duty. A partnership or affiliation with parent-teacher organizations, professional organizations, local zoos or museums, or other venues that already attract your female consumer will enable you to tap into activities or events that your consumers already attend. PTO Today is an interesting organization that has print, online, and event marketing opportunities that connect a brand with millions of involved and enthusiastic parents who have school-age kids. You not only benefit from the credibility associated with those local connections, but also demonstrate your relevance and understanding of these women's busy lives.

One smart organization did just that. We can learn a great deal from the Oxygen Network and its founder and chief executive office, Geraldine Laybourne. Not long ago, Laybourne was speaking at a major conference for female entrepreneurs. She gave the entrepreneurs excellent advice; in particular, her advice to drop the word "multi-tasking" from their vocabulary. Based on the reams of research she has seen, "multi-minding" is much more reflective of women today.

"Using the filter of multi-minding is as important for the Oxygen Network as it is for an entrepreneurial business," she says. "Listen, really listen, to two audiences—your customers and your employees."

Laybourne and her team did just that. A common thread in listening to both business and female consumer audiences was mentoring, a topic that is also a personal passion for Laybourne. She took that nugget of learning and sought to engage it in a meaningful and cost-effective way that would resonate with her key audiences.

And so, the Oxygen Mentoring Initiative was born. Armed with a keen sense of humor and myriad marketing tools at her disposal, Laybourne and her marketing team were able to remake the day of women who were important to them. Not just any women, though. Oxygen successfully reached and engaged high-profile, influential women who have even more hectic schedules, believe it or not, than the average woman.

Kassie Canter, chief communications officer for the Oxygen Network at the time, oversaw the development and birth of the mentoring initiative. The thinking behind the initiative and the way it was implemented was quite smart. We can learn a great deal about how to reach multi-minding women by exploring some of the program's carefully planned elements. When I talked with Canter, she graciously shared the details and we examined why the initiative was so successful.

Oxygen is a network that was built on the premise of being an advocate for women. "From the beginning, the Oxygen brand had a voice and that voice was big and bold," says Canter. "The marketing and communications purposely fell in line with that overall positioning."

From working with the Oxygen team personally, I can tell you they do, indeed, hold their marketing and communications to that standard. They are true to their brand in the big picture and in the details, whether it is a theme for a campaign or the venue for a lunch event.

Remember the Oh! launch campaign? Many women remember this campaign because it was bold, consistent, and simple, but not simplistic. In 2007, the cable network's viewership exceeded 71 million homes with an audience of young, independent women who wanted fun entertainment that challenged stereotypes and made no apologies for it. About 70 percent of Oxygen's viewers are women between the ages of 18 and 49 who are in their prime multi-minding years. That audience represents the fourth-highest concentration of women in that age-group in all of cable television.[5] Oxygen is definitely a brand worthy of our attention.

"When we do research at Oxygen, we try to break down stereotypes," notes Canter.

> For instance, our finance study showed that women are the financial decision makers. They are not just paying bills, but making the major financial decisions in the household. Another study revealed that, contrary to popular belief at the time, women love the use of humor in marketing messages and the humor sticks with them.

Research from *Parenting* magazine confirms that moms like funny messages on weeknights because they need a laugh at the end of the day. Weekends are times when women with children are even more receptive to funny, quirky messaging.[6]

It was Oxygen that led the way in breaking the stereotypes about women and technology. In its Girls Gone Wired study, Oxygen showed that the technology gap has virtually closed and that the majority of women are hungry for technology. True to its mission to be big and bold, the headline of the study was a provocative "Tech is the New Bling."

In fact, the study revealed that 77 percent of women polled would prefer a new plasma television to a diamond solitaire necklace. In addition, the study showed that a full 70 percent of the female market is interested in and is using technology, debunking the myth that men and female urban trendsetters have the predominant interest in technology.[7]

Laybourne notes, "We are proud to be giving women the credit they deserve for being savvy and knowledgeable about technology—something we have long suspected and are thrilled to be able to qualify."

Oxygen's research covered a number of topics over time to give them a deeper knowledge of issues that are important to women. Oxygen's research also showed that while the "old boys' network" is alive and well, women are mentoring women, but struggling with how to work that additional activity into their day. That insight, combined with one chief executive officer's passion, inspired an important program that found a way into women's days and their hearts.

"It really all started when Gerry wanted to help mentor young talent, but needed to find a way to fit it into her day," says Canter.

"Gerry's multi-minding solution—mentoring while taking a walk in Central Park at lunchtime—enabled her time to do double duty. She could get some exercise and provide mentoring advice at the same time. That way, mentoring could fit into her busy day."

Just like this busy chief executive officer found an inventive way to multi-mind and make her day more productive and rewarding, so, too, do many other women. Multi-minding is a coping mechanism, some say an art form, that women have developed to help them more effectively juggle all of the dimensions of their complex lives. When I have talked to and surveyed women of all walks of life, whether they are stay-at-home moms or executives, they all say "that's me" when I describe multi-minding.

Oxygen works hard to know its multi-minding audience well. "Women are complicated," Canter explains. "We've done a lot of research and built many relationships with our audience so we can really understand them. You have to get to them on something that is really important and useful and make it easy at the same time. You can't really know them without hard work."

In addition to being Laybourne's passionate interest, mentoring is an area of particular importance to Oxygen's predominately female audience. Taking on its role of advocate, Oxygen designed a mentoring program that was very much a reflection of Laybourne's model. Never a network to be shy, Oxygen set out to create the "new girls' network" through which women can mentor women in contrast to the still-common "old boys' network," in which men traditionally mentor men.

Large-scale mentoring "walks" were planned and implemented in major cities. The walks engaged high-profile and influential women to walk with and mentor aspiring, young women. Oxygen certainly has its share of connections with high-profile women, but getting influential women from a broad range of careers to commit to a mentoring walk is still a huge challenge. Time is at a super-premium for these women.

"We tried to make it something that would be easy to commit to," recalls Canter, "and we could tell them, based on Gerry's experiences, that they would get something out of this experience, too. It was definitely a two-way street."

That sentiment rang true with influential women, such as actresses Marlo Thomas and Meryl Streep and news anchor Deborah Norville, as well as many female senior executives from a wide range of businesses. The walks received enthusiastic media coverage in the cities where they were held. By covering the events, television and radio stations, local newspapers, and magazines further extended the reach of the initiative. *Good Morning America* even dubbed the initiative "a mentoring program like no other."

True to Oxygen's mission, the walks were big, bold, and uncomplicated, playing directly to busy women who need to get a lot done every day.

Questions Every Marketer or Business Owner Should Ask

- Am I using search engine optimization to reach mass numbers of women online?
- Is there an appropriate way to use humor in communications for my brand or business?
- Are we leveraging our CEO's passion for causes with our female audience?
- Do our events enable our female consumers to do double duty with their time?
- Do we ask for and use the input of local voices when we do local events?

"We designed the mentoring walks so that both the mentor and the mentee get something valuable without having to commit a great deal of time," Canter recalls. "The events are exciting, fun, rewarding and pretty, but very focused."

Canter and her team spent a great deal of time preparing for the events to ensure that the mentor-mentee pairings were matched in the most relevant way. Once the walk was over, Oxygen let the participants manage the mentor-mentee relationships in the best way they saw fit. Different levels of commitment enabled the women to customize their relationship in a way that works for them.

Oxygen knows that one size does not fit all when it comes to women. Therefore, it did not immediately hold walks in several key markets. Instead, the network invited influential women in the city to join them at a lunch. This event planted the idea of women mentoring women in that locale and enabled the network to get ideas from these women on what would work in their area.

In Pittsburgh, I co-hosted the luncheon with Laybourne. The women at the event, high-ranking and influential in their own right, were delighted to spend an hour with other influential women and discuss how the mentoring cause could be furthered. Laybourne and the Oxygen team enthusiastically encouraged idea generation from the group and many suggestions were offered, including the concept of real-time mentoring.

All of the ideas were considered by Oxygen and some of the best were implemented in Pittsburgh. Responding to the need for real-time mentoring, the concept of "mentoring on demand" was born. Oxygen and the local cable operator, Comcast, worked with the influential women to create short mentoring vignettes that aired via Comcast's On Demand channel. This community service channel can be viewed by anyone in the area seeking mentoring advice.

What novel ways to help multi-minding women remake their day—combining mentoring and exercise so time can do double duty; creating an event at which women can eat lunch, network, and do a community service; and providing 24/7 access to mentoring information on a variety of careers. It is no wonder these initiatives were successful with multi-minding women.

Canter cites "word-of-mouth" and "word-of-mouse (online)" as keys to the future of communicating with multi-minding women. "Connect with women offline and online on a topic that's really meaningful and respect that they don't have a lot of time. Women's brains process information in a contextual way. They have a lot they have to get done. Don't overcomplicate your marketing or messages," she recommends.

That's sound advice given that women do not have the time or propensity to entertain commercial messages. Those that quickly connect, as Oxygen does, are much more likely to succeed with female consumers."

Canter predicts the future will bring "years of the woman," when more and more companies ramp up or accelerate their marketing-to-women efforts.

"I think we are over the hump in realizing women are the predominant consumer purchasing force," she notes. "Women are getting credit for the power they have."

Oxygen knows multi-minding women well. Following are the M^2 Must-Dos that you can use to better know your multi-minding female consumers.

M^2 Must-Dos

- ✓ Engage a small group of influentials to seed ideas and to serve as a sounding board.
- ✓ Listen and identify the most credible sources of information for your particular audience and focus attention there—not on trying to reach individual women.
- ✓ Involve your chief executive officer or resident expert in a local market when you want to reinforce the importance of the initiative and of the audience.
- ✓ Focus on key markets where you can build real grassroots support and consistency.
- ✓ Leverage local, editorial media that is considered to be credible in local markets.

Chapter Six

Yes, I Multi-Mind: New Ways to Understand and Reach Multi-Minding Audiences

Women are busy and, let's be honest here, many of us like it that way. Our lives are robust, and while there are certainly moments of insanity, we embrace our filled-to-the-brim lifestyles. We could not live the way we do today if not for our superb mastery of the art of multi-tasking. You know the drill—making breakfast, packing school lunches for the kids, scanning the headlines of the local newspaper, catching a glimpse of a morning show on television, signing a permission slip for a field trip, and packing a briefcase—all at the same time.

Guess what? The activity does not stop there. While the female body is engaged in multi-tasking, the female mind is juggling an endless stream of thoughts. Yes, we multi-mind. In fact, it is a cultural phenomenon that is happening in the homes and minds of most women. It is changing our ability and willingness to receive commercial messages, and it will change the way marketers market to women.

I love talking with women about multi-minding. They get it—immediately and intuitively.

Many women can relate to pausing in the middle of yet another frantic workday while facing a screen full of urgent e-mails, text messages from kids—perhaps one in college asking for money and the other a preteen at home who wants to join MySpace—along with a schedule loaded with afternoon meetings and a half-finished presentation on their laptop.

Decades ago, social trend gurus claimed that evolving technology would so simplify our lives that by the turn of the century, work time would be cut drastically, leaving us with only one challenge: how to spend our abundant "leisure time." What were they thinking?

MOVE OVER MULTI-TASKING

What this all boils down to is that women, especially those between the ages of 25 and 54, are busier than ever juggling their lives at work and at home. This requires not only expert multi-tasking, but also multi-minding.

By now, you know what multi-minding means. Women have bypassed multi-tasking, and are constantly mentally managing the many dimensions of their lives. Their minds are always "on" and flipping through thoughts faster than a man can scan television channels with a remote control.

Numerous studies and just about any woman you ask can attest to the fact that the average working woman spends almost twice as much time as a working man on household chores and care of children. That is not exactly hot, breaking news to most women, even though women are now represented in the workforce nearly as much as men—78 percent of women compared with 85 percent of men have jobs outside the home.

TIME COMPRESSION LEAVES LITTLE ROOM FOR MARKETING

Our lives have evolved along with technology, all right. Technology has, in fact, blurred the boundaries between work and home. Social changes hold women to high standards of performance in both arenas.

Multi-minding, which has come about in this era of time compression, means that female consumers have little or no time for commercial messages. Even at leisure, women's minds are hard at work, making it less likely than in the past that a woman is paying full attention to a television program or commercial. She is also less likely to spend much time reading a long newspaper or magazine article.

Indeed, some media have responded to the fast pace of life today. Many newspapers have changed their design and format, for example, to make news more quickly and easily accessible. Look at the formats of iVillage and *USA Today*, for example. The stories are in bite-size pieces that can quickly be scanned, which is perfect for a busy, multi-minding woman. Take a look, too, at all of the split screens that appear on television stations. You can get a variety of information, such as headlines, weather, sports, and breaking news, all at the same time. Perfect.

REAL SIMPLE IS REALLY EFFECTIVE

Numerous women's magazines have responded to the challenge of today's multi-minding woman by shortening articles and by adding more boxed items and news briefs. *Real Simple* magazine is a prime example and one of the first to really embrace simplicity of layout and content. It is no wonder so many women love it.

Some areas, like traditional, 30-second commercials on television, have lagged behind, however. Traditional advertising works when someone has time to pay attention, but most women do not have that sort of luxury. More marketers are waking up to that reality.

PURCHASING POWER POWERED BY TECHNOLOGY

Marketers are becoming more aware of this reality because women in the multi-minding ages of 25 to 54 have never wielded so much power in the marketplace. They are choosing nearly 85 percent of every disposable dollar that is spent and we are not just talking about laundry soap, groceries, and other household items. Women make the primary spending choices on 53 percent of stock purchases, 63 percent of personal computer buys, and 75 percent of over-the-counter drug sales. They buy half of all new vehicles and are major consumers in other areas traditionally dominated by men. For instance, women are buying 61 percent of major home improvement products and are involved in 89 percent of all consumer electronics decisions.[1]

Beyond the statistics, the fact is that women consumers cannot be underestimated in either importance or sophistication. Not only is multi-minding making some traditional advertising approaches obsolete, but women's use of technology is also changing the rules. Smart, savvy, time-challenged women today are not as dependent on traditional media for buying information. The Internet has become a major factor in purchasing decisions with nearly 90 percent of women surveyed reporting they do more product research online than offline.

In addition to *BusinessWeek* online, many media outlets have picked up on the topic of multi-minding. In fact, I was quite taken aback by the attention it has received from mainstream media and trade publications to blogs and personal response e-mails. *Fast Company Magazine*, *BRANDWEEK* magazine, the *Associated Press*, the *Chicago Tribune*, and others have written about the phenomenon.

The national coverage sparked responses from women who have written about it in their blogs and who have sent me e-mails in response. The personal e-mails, in particular, have indicated to me how multi-minding really does resonate with women and their daily lives. Take a read:

> I feel like you've walked into my home and described my entire lifestyle.… I certainly do not have time for the average advertisement and in the past couple of years have not sat in front of the TV without some sort of professional reading material on my laptop. Thanks to TiVo, I haven't watched a commercial in months.

Here is another personal response to multi-minding:

> A woman selling vacuum cleaners knocked on my door the other day. My husband answered and told me she wanted to speak with me, being the woman of the house. When I came to the door, she proceeded with her sales pitch, which included a

statement that I would get more efficient use out of it than any other vacuum I might have and that its design was easier for women to maneuver. I proceeded to inform her that just because I am a woman does not mean my role is housecleaning. While it is true that I tend to vacuum more than my husband, I certainly didn't appreciate her assumption that housecleaning was my responsibility. When I told my husband about it, he laughed, knowing full well that a sales pitch geared towards old-fashioned women was not the way to reach my pocketbook.

MAJOR IMPLICATIONS OF MULTI-MINDING

Statistics bring to life the experiences you just read. According to a national survey commissioned by MTV Networks, consumers are doing more than 24 hours worth of activity in one day, leading to the assumption that any one activity receiving undivided attention is becoming unlikely. Whether we try to pack 38 hours of activity into a day as the Yahoo! research suggests or just more than 24 hours as MTV notes, it just is not possible unless we are multi-minding.

Let's explore some of the dimensions of multi-minding in more detail, as these details reveal how to connect with multi-minding consumers. Research done in recent years by the Ketchum Global Research Network shows the following:

- Women 25 to 54 are 31 percent more likely than men to say they juggle a lot of tasks (81 percent of women versus 62 percent of men) and are 22 percent more likely to say they juggle a lot of thoughts (72 percent of women versus 59 percent of men).

The point is not that women or men are better than each other at handling more tasks or for being more focused. The point is that the two are different and we must realize this critical point when marketing to women. We cannot or will not give undivided attention to most things, especially marketing, and that means your marketing will be hit or miss unless you surround her—more to come on that topic in chapter 12. If you are really interested in that topic, go to chapter 12 now and dig in while you are thinking about it.

- Three-quarters of women 25 to 54 agree that many things are competing for their attention at the same time (74 percent), which is 23 percent higher than men 25 to 54 (60 percent).

Marketers are vying for women's attention. Add that to the dozens of family, personal, and work items that we have on our long list of things to do. No wonder we are tired at the end of the day after wading through so many items all screaming, "Look at me!" In order to survive, women must ignore the things that are not priorities or, if possible, put them on the back burner until time can be devoted to them. The keys are communicating to her via credible sources (and she will tell you who they are) and being there when she's ready.

- Three-quarters of women 25 to 54 agree they spend more time thinking about others' needs than their own (74 percent), a difference of 51 percent from men in general (49 percent).

When I saw this finding, women's vast and growing purchasing power came into focus. We buy on behalf of our families and for ourselves, most often in that order. We think about what our family likes to eat and, 90 percent of the time, we shop for the groceries. We think about and research our family's needs for a vehicle and 62 percent of the time, we buy the vehicle. Women control $3.3 trillion in consumer spending and that figure, according to *BusinessWeek* magazine, will continue to increase.

As women's purchasing power grows to new levels, so will the amount of marketing aimed at this particular audience. That is why it is so very important to understand how to reach them.

THE NEW EXPERTS: FRIENDS AND FAMILY

If you remember nothing else, note that experts, friends and family, and media reports are the three most credible sources of information for women and that friends and family are cited as the most credible sources of information when making a purchasing decision.

To me, this is the holy grail for communicating with female consumers. Reach her via credible sources, and when she is ready to buy, she will come your way. The impact of friends and family as credible sources has grown over the years. In fact, in the 18 months between Ketchum's two research studies, friends and family moved from the second most credible source to the top most credible source of information for women making a purchasing decision.

To some extent, "girls' nights out" are really product research sessions. Try that one on your husband or boyfriend. And, all of those poolside chats during the heat of the summer are actually preparation for back-to-school buying. Daily phone calls from your sister or mom? They are one of the single biggest influences in what you will buy next.

That means marketers need to give our friends and family things to talk about. Interestingly, the Ketchum research showed that after friends and family, the next top 10 sources that female consumers turn to are not "commercial" sources, but rather experts: consumer opinion

Web sites, magazines, local television news, local newspapers, shopping Web sites that include reviews, national television news, brand and store Web sites, national newspapers, and radio news.

Notice a great deal of "news" on that list? That means we need to create real news that can be commented on by experts and covered in consumer media to give friends and family something to talk about. That means public relations should play a huge role moving forward in tapping the buying power of today's multi-minding female consumer.

Women have little time for commercial messages, but they will create time for messages that are important to them and delivered by a credible source (remember—friends and family). Even the advertising industry and major marketers are admitting that women simply are not buying into the messages they have to sell.

Understanding the life of a typical female consumer, is it surprising that a 30-second ad is not working like it used to? Think about what you are doing while an ad is running on television, if you do not have TiVo and actually are watching the ad. Perhaps you are also planning dinner, calling in a prescription, checking out a recipe online, doing laundry, and looking to see whether the kids are still playing in the back yard. How much time or attention is the ad getting? Virtually none. Yet, marketers still spend hundreds of millions of dollars to deliver their messages to consumers' homes via such communications.

WHAT MARKETERS MUST DO

How do we reach this increasingly vital and decreasingly attentive group of consumers? There are solutions that meet the challenges of marketing to the multi-minding consumer.

We need simply to start asking her questions instead of assuming we know all the answers. Women are a diverse group and one size does not fit all. They include baby boomers and Gen Yers, mothers of young children, those whose kids have left the nest, and women who are not parents at all. They are women with traditionally female as well as non-traditional jobs, professionals, and blue-collar workers. They embrace a myriad of ethnicities and cultures and a wide range of political beliefs. One size, quite definitively, does not fit all. Focus groups and surveys are more crucial than ever in helping to determine what women want.

Earlier in this book, Mimi Doe talked about literally "sitting in their circle." Conducting focus groups in women's homes, as Procter & Gamble has done, really gets to those critical nuances. Such tactics help to go beyond the quantitative surveys. Make sure such focus groups are more representative of the increasingly diverse segments within the audience known as "women."

Accommodate the demands on her time and attention. Timeliness, credibility, and relevance to her busy life are keys to capturing women's attention. Marketers need to get to the point and give vital information in a way that will make women want to listen. Remember the door-to-door vacuum sales example earlier in this chapter? That company has a lot to learn.

Embrace holistic approaches. Want to make the short list of her choices? Weave your information and messages within the complicated fabric of a woman's life by letting her know what is available, informing her why and how it meets her needs, and subtly communicating throughout the busy hours of her life via whispers, not shouts, and through Web site content development, as well as more traditional media.

Take the female consumer seriously. My grandmother used to say she has "more time than money." Today, more women have the money but not the time. She is making primary decisions on major purchases with increasing frequency. She is also quick to turn off or tune out any advertising message that is perceived as old-fashioned, offensive, silly, or otherwise lacking in credibility. Time is too short. Fail to give her the vital information she needs right now and she will quickly go elsewhere.

JUST ASK SOME WOMEN

As I was writing this book, I launched a blog, Toobusytoshop. blogspot.com, to capture input and insights from real women to complement the portfolio of expert interviews that I have included. I asked women to comment on the topics of multi-minding and collecting credible opinions (which I call CROPing), and to explain how marketers can make their multi-minding lives easier. Here is the premise of the blog:

Are You Too Busy To Shop?

This blog will help me collect input from women for my upcoming book, *Too Busy to Shop: Marketing to Multi-Minding Women*. I'd love to hear from you!

Women today are busier than ever, including me. Multi-tasking has evolved into multi-minding as we physically and mentally juggle the many dimensions of our complex lives. All of that activity leaves little time for commercial messages. And that means, dare I say it, I am too busy to shop.

Yet, as the primary purchaser for my household, I need and want to buy. How does a marketer reach me? That's a tough one. But, based on my busy lifestyle, I can tell you what works for me and what doesn't. Perhaps if we share our thoughts and experiences, we can help marketers manage their brands and businesses so they work with our busy lives, not against them.

The input I received has been enlightening, funny, and helpful to me, and I think the perspectives and examples also will be helpful to marketers. Following are some selected references and examples, as well as implications, which I have provided for marketers and business owners.

First, it is important to note that via a poll on my blog, 100 percent of respondents say they are "constantly" multi-minding, even when given the options of specifying that they do so "only when I am really busy" and "every once in a while." The concept of multi-minding has played out in formal research and its impact is supported by the input of real women responding to my blog. Multi-minding is certainly a pervasive phenomenon and one of the biggest challenges facing marketers today.

SHE'LL SPEND MONEY, BUT DON'T MAKE HER SPEND HER TIME

When I asked women how multi-minding affects their ability to shop, the phrase "too busy to shop" sprang to life in vivid ways. Women told me they truly are too busy to shop and instead are engaging all types of tips and tools to help them manage their daily lives. Following are a few highlights worth sharing.

One of my first posts was about exercise:

It's that time of the year ... swimsuit season is just a few months away. We are looking to shed a few pounds and trying to get in shape. Who has the time or the desire to think about new, more healthful foods, a new exercise routine, new exercise equipment, a gym membership?

Add this to the consideration list. I was listening to a fitness instructor who said you should not do the same workout day after day. You need to "surprise" your muscles.

Maybe all of you know this already, but my Comcast On Demand channels now include dozens of fitness and sports training activities. On Saturday, bored with my Stairmaster and threatened by the guy who implied the almost-daily Stairmaster routine won't surprise my body enough to help fitness, I discovered (OK, my husband showed me) the on-demand options. I was intrigued by the Navy Seals training modules and guess what— they are seven to eight minutes long! Perfect. Did the stretching module and felt proud. Now, I am in Navy Seals training.

I received some great responses, including the following: "Try Jorge Cruise's 8 Minutes in the Morning workout—fun, fast, and effective" and "I do a 10-minute Pilates routine with a Pilates video. I can make room in my day for a 10-minute workout and the kids usually do it along with me." I also heard from a woman whose gym now offers classes and activities for kids, so mom can go to the gym with her kids and get a workout in, while her kids work out a bit and have fun.

A number of implications emerge here for marketers and business owners. To say that time is at a premium is a gross understatement. These women are time-starved, trying to pack 38 hours of activity into a 24-hour day. Help them by offering products and services that can be accessed or accomplished quickly. Attach a time expectation to your brand and stick to it.

Given these examples, women with children want and expect that companies or products will accommodate their children. These women want to spend time with their children and need ways to help them do it. If your brand or business is targeted to moms, incorporate some accommodation for their children. Offer mini-manicures at the hair salon, provide mini-shopping carts at the grocery store, or place cartoon strips on the inside label of a food product. Help moms be the best they can by spending more time with their kids.

Notice, too, the specific brand mentions. When women like something, they are not afraid to share it with others. This blog, as other blogs, social networks, and Web sites do, serves as a filter to brands capable of driving consumers to or away from your brand or business. Do not underestimate the filter power of blogs and online sites. Engage those blogs and sites in genuine relationship-building activities just as you would a consumer. They have the power to reach and influence thousands of your key consumers.

This post about grocery stores elicited a number of responses:

> Here I am, a multi-minding woman with lots on my mind. Important stuff like what really good, nutritious meal can I put on the table quickly when I get home at 6:30 after work. That's what I'm thinking as I enter my local grocery store. That, and should I let my four-year-old daughter use the handheld bar code scanner, which will take 12 minutes longer, or do I stand in line at the checkout and have to take my groceries out of the cart twice? Yes, for the sake of time, I debate that kind of stuff, along with do I spend five minutes standing in line at the deli today.
>
> Walking into the store, I realize I have a new challenge. They are rearranging the aisles. Not just a few product lines, but the entire inner section! I can't believe it. With daughter in tow, I have to search out every item … for weeks! I am not happy. I can't plan my shopping list by the store layout. I can no longer breeze through aisles knowing where everything is. It takes me 23 minutes more to get what I need. If I had a reasonable alternative, I'd switch stores.
>
> Rearranging more than two aisles at a time in the grocery store is an enemy of the busy woman and should be illegal.

Here is a sampling of the responses. "I have shopping down to a science and I detest anything that slows down my process. I can relate." One woman noted how frustrating it can be when she needs to quickly run into a store on a busy night, only to find the familiar setup has been changed. "My post-work runaround included picking up cupcakes, cooking dinner, attending a meeting, homework supervision—all while my husband is traveling." Her multi-tasking, multi-minding evening did not need any curve balls.

THE DELI DILEMMA

One response, in particular, was so entertaining that I want to share it in its entirety. It is called the "Deli Dilemma."

I welcome the time-saving feature of the self-service kiosk at the deli. I can quickly type in my order—dexterity is one of my strong attributes. As the order is processed, I am happily multi-tasking by shopping for other groceries. However, the majority of the time, I find there is an attractive, professionally made, white paper sign with hand-written, black Sharpie letters posted on the kiosk that boldly announces "Out Of Order." Meanwhile, under the sign, I can hear the kiosk welcoming me to place an order. The situation exasperates me.

My conspiracy theory is that the part-time deli clerks don't want the extra work load of processing the kiosk orders. Unlike multi-minding ladies, they have all the time in the world—they are *at* work. There is no incentive to process orders more efficiently, so why bother. As my blood pressure rises because I see precious time being wasted, I grudgingly grab a number. Typically, there is a six- to eight-person wait. So, in the nearby aisles, I frantically search for soda, juice, and snacks while periodically checking the rotation of numbers. And, God forbid if you miss your number. It's like a mortal sin trying to regain pole position!

Once my number is bellowed, I wait again for the clerk to open the package of meat (never fails there's not one open), slice it to my liking, package it, and ask for the next item. In addition, I especially enjoy the chitchat amongst the clerks—wasting more of my time. Meanwhile, my multi-mind is thinking about finishing this daunting task and returning home to spend time with my family. Overall, I guess the deli trip is worth it because my kids enjoy lunches packed by mom that include little love notes. (Maria T. Brady, mompreneur, marketing agency owner and jewelry gallery partner.)

A valuable lesson can be learned from these great examples. Do not slow her down, especially when you provide a tool, like the self-serve

Questions Every Marketer or Business Owner Should Ask

- Are you capturing the input and opinions of your highest-value consumers and using that input to change and enhance your marketing?

- Are you engaging sources that women deem to be credible to deliver your messages?

- Are you working with blogs, Web sites, and social networking sites so they can serve as filters for your brand or business?

- Are you developing holistic ideas that reach women in a comprehensive and meaningful way?

- What time-saving benefit does your brand or business offer? How do you inform and engage women about that benefit?

- Does your brand or business slow down a woman's day?

---

deli machine, that is intended to help her save time. It is one of the single largest frustrations I have heard from women. Online e-tailers should make it fast and easy to order items, and do not force consumers to enter a slew of information every time they revisit the site. Grocery stores should provide online ordering and delivery options, have enough check-outs open and make sure your self-serve deli machine is always operating correctly. Salons should take customers on time and give them a hand massage if the hair stylist is running behind schedule. Every brand or business should be able to add a time-saving element that benefits female consumers.

WOMEN SHOP FOR OTHERS FIRST AND OFTEN

An interesting take on having time to shop is that many women make time to shop for others, but not for themselves. This feedback is consistent with research I have seen that indicates multi-minding women think of others' needs first, and they do so 75 percent of the time. The entire premise of my blog is devoted to women not having time to shop anymore. Here is proof of that premise from a response to my blog:

> I love your blog and will send it around to all of my friends— the concept is so true. We're having my baby's baptism on Easter in Atlanta. The baby has numerous ensembles; I made sure my husband has a new suit weeks ago. Of course, this weekend, I finally found something for myself in 20 minutes while my husband waited for me with the baby. Leisurely shopping is over for me.

Reaching today's time-challenged women by listening to their needs, keeping up with trends, and surrounding them with useful information via new media sources that are congruent with their complex lifestyle is vital. To lag behind and to do less with today's powerful, techno-savvy, multi-minding female consumers just does not make sense.

M^2 Must-Dos

✓ Ask her what she needs or wants instead of assuming you know.

✓ Accommodate the demands on her time and attention.

✓ Embrace holistic approaches.

✓ Take the female consumer seriously.

✓ Attach a time expectation to your brand and stick to it.

✓ If targeting moms, also accommodate their children's needs.

Chapter Seven

Before Women Shop, They CROP: The CRedible OPinions Shortcut

Ads, elaborate in-store displays, and an ongoing monologue from an eager salesman all competed for Sara's attention at the local Best Buy. A happily married 38-year-old teacher with two school-age kids and a busy lifestyle, Sara approached the electronics counter with confidence. She distinctly remembered the details of a recent conversation with her best friend, who had recommended a particular camera because of the ease of the online photo-management site.

Her friend knew online photo management was a priority for Sara, whose many nondigital photos were stuffed into shoe boxes under every bed in the house. After that conversation, Sara scanned the ratings guide from *Consumer Reports* and remembering her best friend's great experience with her new digital camera, she quickly found the camera that she had come seeking.

"I'll take that one," she said, interrupting the salesman's technology-laden monologue as he moved into the area of more expensive cameras. "This is the digital camera that I want."

What most influences a woman's buying decisions? Ads? Celebrities? A mention in the media? Actually, family and friends prove to be the most significant shopping influencers, according to a survey by Ketchum.

BEFORE SHE ENTERS THE STORE

Like many women today, Sara had researched her purchase thoroughly before setting foot in the store. She's quite typical of today's multiminding woman who is constantly thinking about and preparing for the multiple dimensions of her life while pursuing everyday activities.

With more decision-making and purchasing power than ever before, today's busy 25- to 54-year-old woman is using a valuable shortcut before she sets out to purchase a product, be it consumer electronics, consumer-packaged goods, or food for her family. She will CROP before she shops.

What does it mean to CROP?

This is an important new trend: women seek CRedible OPinions while researching potential purchases. As such, it is an essential short-cut to purchases.

When CROPing, women trim research time by consulting a few close friends and family members, as well as experts, local news, and magazines. These people offer credible opinions by validating research and helping to determine buying decisions; it is the intersection of two hot marketing topics—word-of-mouth and influencers.

WHO DOES A WOMAN BELIEVE?

With little time for commercial messages and less time than ever for recreational shopping, today's women research purchases by seeking information—first, from family and friends; then from experts, such as nutritionists, chefs, or doctors; and, finally, from consumer ratings and Web sites (see table 7.1). Experts ranked second in credibility for infor-mation on consumer-packaged goods and food, but ranked third behind consumer ratings and Web sites for consumer electronic products.

Ninety-one percent of women surveyed say friends and family give "very" or "somewhat" credible information in advising them on buying decisions for consumer-packaged goods, consumer electronics, and food. This finding can prove critical to marketers who are eager to determine what influences women between the ages of 25 and 54, the key decision makers in the family, despite being pressed for time.

For multi-minding women, the ability to CROP enables them to save precious time while researching their purchases, something most women do before buying.

PREPURCHASE RESEARCH PROVIDES BIG SELLING OPPORTUNITY

The trend toward prepurchase research via credible opinion seeking was discovered during an April 2006 study I conducted with the Ketchum Global Research Network that targeted a sample of 1,500 women ages 25 to 54. This sample, representative of today's busy, multi-tasking, and multi-minding American woman, revealed three par-ticularly interesting findings for marketers:[1]

- First, more than half of women research consumer-packaged goods and food purchases "some" or "a lot" before heading to the store. Some 80 percent of these women reported doing advance research for consumer electronic purchases.

Table 7.1 Friends and Family Top the Credible Sources List for Women Across the Verticals
Percent of Respondents Who Answered "Very" or "Somewhat" Credible.

	Food	Consumer Electronics	Consumer-Packaged Goods
Friends and family	91%	91%	91%
Experts (e.g., doctors, chefs, in-store personnel, etc.)	86%	81%	82%
Consumer opinion/ratings Web sites	77%	84%	79%
Magazine article	72%	73%	72%
Local TV news	71%	72%	72%
Local newspaper	70%	68%	70%
Shopping Web sites that include user reviews	70%	79%	74%
National TV news	68%	70%	69%
Brand/store Web sites	65%	69%	65%
National newspaper	65%	67%	66%
Radio news	60%	61%	62%
Advertising	57%	54%	57%
Direct mail	48%	46%	49%
Entertainment	42%	43%	44%
Blogs, forums, or usenets	40%	43%	41%

Source: Ketchum Global Research Network, Women 25 to 54 Study, 2006.

- Second, seeking credible opinions is a major part of this research. Family and friends are the most trusted of credible opinion sources across all product categories; with 91 percent of the women surveyed saying this information was "very" or "somewhat" credible and helpful in their buying decisions. The women also found the opinions of experts and consumer opinion or rating information sources to be credible, although less so than input from family and friends, in their buying decisions.
- Third, "influencers," who are most likely to spread the word about products and services, are primarily women in this same important 25 to 54 age-group. These women are most often married mothers who are employed outside the home and whose busy lives have prompted them to value the opinions they get from trusted sources as a shortcut to making buying decisions. These influencers also have the means and the

Table 7.2   Seven in 10 Women Research Big Purchases
Question: On a scale of 1 to 5, Where 1 is strongly disagree and 5 is strongly agree, how much do you agree with the following statements?

	Strongly Agree or Agree	Strongly Disagree or Disagree
I do research before making big purchases.	72%	8%
I rarely make impulsive purchases.	35%	30%
I'm one of the first to try new products and services.	25%	44%
Brand image is important to me.	20%	49%

Source: Ketchum Global Research, Women 25 to 54 Survey, 2006.

confidence to try new products and then pass on information about the value of these products to their own family and friends.

When making purchasing decisions, women want to make informed decisions and are likely to spend more time researching large purchases. Take a look at table 7.2 about the amount of research women do when making major purchases.

The majority of women surveyed conduct research, yet do not have the time to do exhaustive research themselves from scratch. Therefore, they must take shortcuts and get reliable information at the same time. They start CROPing to facilitate their multi-minding lifestyle.

RELATIONSHIPS ARE CENTRAL TO SUCCESS

Who *are* these increasingly savvy women who CROP before they shop?

Women have a lot on their minds and their plates are overflowing, but they make time for things that are important to them. Many women claim they rarely have enough free time and that their daily to-do lists include more tasks than they can accomplish. The research at Ketchum found that relationships are at the center of their busy lives. A woman's definition of success is focused on the quality of her relationships, including her marriage and her relationships with children and other family members.

Good health (both her own and that of her family members) is also high on the list of defining success factors. These two measures of success are intertwined with good relationships, which are considered an important component of wellness. Although fewer than half of those surveyed felt their health had improved in the past five years, the majority expressed interest in reading and learning valuable information about health and nutrition to make the best possible wellness-related lifestyle and purchasing decisions.

Another important finding about these women: they are busy by choice. They have positive feelings about their many responsibilities at home and at work and value the goal of a balanced life. The majority of those surveyed (69 percent) reported being able to make time to savor life's pleasures. For those who felt their lives needed more balance, not enough free time and not having time to themselves were major complaints. Saving time in daily tasks is a top priority, and that is where CROPing appears to be a major shortcut to making smart buying decisions in an increasingly complicated marketplace.

PLANT THE SEEDS FOR ORGANIC CROPING

How can companies best reach women in this important target audience? An "organic" approach to reaching these women is critical to success. That is, messages must be integrated into the context of women's lives and information systems rather than being sent as a barrage of life-interrupting direct messages to the consumer.

I use the word organic to describe efforts that are a natural part of women's lives. There has been quite a bit of research and study about this concept. Forrester Research defines organic branding in this way:

> Brands that connect with their target consumers must be more organic in nature: They must align more closely with their core consumer and be developed and nurtured by those consumers, as well as by the companies that market them. Consumers have an unprecedented ability to broadcast their brand experiences. Companies that harness that ability and use it to create organic brands will find a way to market that keeps their brand equity and brand dignity firmly intact.[2]

With this organic approach in mind, a variety of ways can impact the buying decisions of women today by tapping into the CROPing dynamic. Based on the experience and research I have seen, major themes have emerged in areas where women seem to engage CROPing to facilitate their research and to make purchasing decisions.

HEALTH AND WELLNESS NO LONGER THE DOMAIN OF DOCTORS

For example, women's interest in and concerns about health and wellness have reached an all-time high. Whether the topic is pregnancy or prescription drugs, diets, or disease, women are turning to those who can provide the most credible opinions not only because they are trusted opinions, but also because they are filters that provide needed shortcuts in a world burdened with endless information. What is interesting is that the most sought-after credible opinions, even in the health-and-wellness space, are no longer just those from experts, doctors, or health care professionals.

Research and anecdotal experiences show that increasingly, the most credible source for women is peers and other like-minded women. According to research conducted by Thecradle.com, an emerging group of moms is shying away from the exalted expert and even the popular "alpha moms." Instead, a new segment of women are gaining the confidence to trust their own maternal instincts and the wisdom of other women who are at a similar life stage. This research reveals that new and expectant mothers are seeking other "experts," namely, their peers, and trusting their own instincts. Nearly 80 percent of the 3,000 or so respondents to The Cradle's survey said they are involved in an online social community, and one in four pregnant women said she participates in or reads online message boards.

With peers—online and offline—playing such an influential role in providing prepurchase credible opinions, brands and businesses would be wise to tap into peer networks. In the category of health and wellness, companies like WeightWatchers are building online communities into their Web sites. The communities provide message boards, a recipe exchange, and an open forum for like-minded consumers who are managing their weight in a similar way.

IN-STORE FRUSTRATION HAS LED TO MORE CROPING

Another category in which women used to turn to experts, usually in the store, is consumer electronics. Today, women increasingly are turning to friends, family, and online research sources to explore options and do their homework before they even enter the store. The motivation for CROPing in the consumer electronics space is a bit different than it is for other categories. While many women say buying consumer electronic products is "easy," those in the baby boomer segment of this target population, as well as those with the least amount of free time, are likely to find consumer electronics shopping most exasperating because of the frustrating in-store experience.

The frustration stems from feelings that they are being talked down to, technical jargon obscures the product or service benefits, and the product is not described in a way that relates to women's lives. For example, the sales person may provide information about bytes in reference to a product's memory capability, but it would be more effective to describe memory in terms of how many pictures of kids can be saved. Poor in-store experiences have driven women to talk to like-minded women, online and offline, before they enter the store. Equipped with knowledge that is meaningful to their lifestyle, more women are making their purchasing decisions in advance of the retail experience and are using the store just to complete the transaction of that predetermined choice.

As mentioned, research shows that 7 in 10 women do their research before making big purchases. While they do research, multi-minding women are also looking for those valuable shortcuts that can save time. They go CROPing before they go shopping. Brands or businesses that sell or represent items deemed to be big purchases should be keenly aware of CROPing and how their brand is interacting with and influencing peers of their target consumers.

Women are more likely to make an impulse purchase with less costly or everyday items, but they still engage CROPing even for commoditized products. Think of the millions of women enrolled in the pregnancy and new mom communities on sites like iVillage, the Huggies Baby Network, or Urbanbaby.com. The conversation threads cover every topic and product category imaginable ranging from spas and sport utility vehicles to baby wipes and toilet paper.

Every day, millions of women are being influenced by opinions they believe to be credible. As much as 90 percent of the time for many categories, women deem their family and friends, or peers, to be the most credible source of opinions. Pay close attention to this CROPing trend and find more ways to incorporate word-of-mouth campaigns to engage this audience.

EDITORIAL MEDIA PROVIDES FODDER FOR CROPING

In addition to family and friends emerging as the most credible source of information for women, the credible sources chart in this chapter suggests another important communications finding. You'll notice that 10 of the top 12 most credible sources of information pertain to "editorial" news, both national and local. Whether television, print, or radio, nonadvertising editorial information is deemed to be significantly credible. Those stories women see on the local television news or read in a national magazine are quite credible to them.

Many of the clients and companies that I work with have been surprised to learn how important local editorial news is to women. Local television news and local newspapers are cited ahead of national television news and national newspapers in terms of being credible sources. Oddly enough, many clients still come to public relations firms asking for help in getting media coverage on the national morning shows or in newspapers like *USA Today*.

The credible sources chart indicates, however, that marketers should be paying more, not less, attention to key local markets and the media in those markets. While having a product appear on or in a national media outlet has a certain cachet, the female consumer actually finds more value in having the product appear in a local media venue.

I believe the editorial news, both local and national, is feeding and shaping those credible opinions of friends and family. It is serving as the fodder for conversation, along with the many highly regarded online communities.

VIRTUAL FRIENDS AND FAMILY ARE VERY INFLUENTIAL

Speaking of online communities, the research I have seen leads me to believe that women view trusted online communities and sites as "friends and family," albeit virtual friends and family. That is, when women cite peers or friends and family as the most credible sources of information, they seem to be referring to friends and family in terms of real and virtual.

A recent article in *Forbes* magazine, dubbed "The New Back Fence," describes what is happening with friends and family online through social networking sites like CafeMom.com. The members of CafeMom use the site to make friends and seek support. Launched less than two years ago, Cafemom.com is one of the newer social networking sites for moms and is also one of the fastest-growing sites.

Marketers are flocking to leverage the site with banner ads, sponsorships, discussion forums, and promotions. The Cafemom.com members seem to relish the attention. "What a blessing!" one mom wrote after receiving a Playskool kit that was sent to members of a birthday party discussion group.[3] These women are CROPing, using Cafemom. com as a filter for trusted opinions for a range of products and services.

A recent article in the *Wall Street Journal* detailed how the MySpace generation is using online polls to help plan weddings. "These couples are part of a Web generation accustomed to sharing minute-by-minute details of their personal lives online and getting instant feedback and comments from friends."[4] In other words, they are CROPing. Before deciding which type and flavor of cake to purchase or which wedding attendant gown to buy, these consumers are getting credible opinions in an instant from their online friends and family.

Major marketers, like Disney and Johnson & Johnson, are courting influential bloggers, who have become an online extension of friends and family, like they used to woo traditional national media. Press releases, conferences, and special events, once the domain of only the most influential media, are now being used to connect with bloggers. For example, Johnson & Johnson hosted 56 influential mommy bloggers to an all-expense-paid trip to a three-day conference in New Jersey called Camp Baby. The intent was to forge a stronger bond with moms.

SEARCH-POWERED ANSWERS

Another vital tool in online CROPing is search engines. The power of search engines is undeniable. According to the 2007 Media Usage Survey conducted by Ketchum and the University of Southern California, 69 percent of women use search engines, compared to 66 percent of men. Search engines are the frontline in online CROPing activity.

One of my colleagues at Ketchum, Gur Tsabar, vice president and new media strategist, has a name for online search activity among the virtual friends and family of moms. He calls it the "Googling mom" phenomenon. In an article in Ketchum's online magazine, *Perspectives*, Tsabar writes,

> Mothers are known for searching for solutions—whether it's a recipe for a quick meal or a way to stop the kids from fighting. But a certain kind of mom is in a constant state of searching. Instinctively, she seeks out answers for herself, her family and others. She is the "Googling mom." Predictably, search engines are one of her primary tools.... Women, in general, tend to use search engines slightly more than men, but the Googling mom does more than use search engines. She treats online resources like friends and family—turning to the Web for wisdom on questions that she is certain someone must have had before her.[5]

Across all segments, online activities are integrated heavily into moms' lives, according to a recent, year-long study by MindShare, a media planning and buying powerhouse. Three of the top five sources of information for moms are online, including Internet news and research, which ranked number one; e-mail, which ranked third; and Internet transactions, which ranked fifth. True to what has been found in several other studies, talking to friends and family and reading daily newspapers are included in the top five sources of information.[6]

CROPING IN ACTION

Multi-minding women have little or no time for commercial messages. They spend less time at single-focused pursuits, like recreational shopping or watching television. Fewer women than ever are browsing shopping malls, and when watching television or cooking dinner, they may be working online simultaneously.

Questions Every Marketer or Business Owner Should Ask

- Who is my target consumer turning to for credible opinions?
- Is my brand or business actively engaging those credible sources?
- Am I engaging local and national editorial media for my brand or business?
- What is the process my female consumer uses to research my product or service? How can I make it easier and more productive for her?
- Am I connecting with blogs and social networking sites that serve as filters to my consumer? What are their perceptions of my brand or business?
- When a woman uses a search engine for my brand or category, what does she see? Am I fully optimizing search engines for my brand or business?

What women will make time for and even seek are the opinions of trusted sources, most often friends and family. You certainly could test women you know and come up with similar conclusions. Through research done at Ketchum, through personal experiences, and via my blog, (Toobusytoshop.blogspot.com), I collected input from women on how and when they CROP. You will be fascinated and learn a great deal by reading the following real-life examples of how these women CROP.

Following is one of my posts and some typical responses:

Too Busy to Blog

Sorry for the delay in creating this latest post. I've been too busy to blog. I've heard from a number of you about how and when you CROP, or look for CRedible Opinions, as a shortcut to purchase because we are all too busy to do all of the research ourselves. Many women turn to friends and family—sisters, moms, and close friends online and offline—to get recommendations.

For example, my sister knows everyone in the world and can quickly recommend anything from the quickest place to get X-rays to the best place to get prepared salad.

Who do you turn to and for what? Let me know.

Here are some quotes that bring the CROPing dynamic to life:

Everything I do is online ... I could never leave the house. Yikes! Remember that prediction in the first chapter about empty parking lots? It may already be happening, so what are you doing about seizing opportunities and managing relationships with your highest-value customers online?

I feel like you've walked into my home and described my entire lifestyle.

The concepts of multi-minding and CROPing are, indeed, resonating with women. Women themselves have created these mind-sets and patterns of behavior. I just described what I saw in action in the marketplace. What is more important at this point are the implications for marketing and how marketers manage these new dynamics. The rest of this book provides insights, examples, and predictions for the new world of marketing to women.

Reaching today's busy woman is an issue we deal with daily here at X Corporation.

More effectively marketing to today's multi-minding woman is truly at the top of the list of many businesses and brands today. The marketplace is changing as we speak and as you read this book. That is why marketing to women must be a continuous learning process. It is a journey, not a destination.

What an eloquent way of saying what many of us have been thinking for years. More often than not, I use 38 hours worth of a day—not 24!

As women pack so much activity into one day, as evidenced by this quote, they must take shortcuts in helping them make purchasing decisions. There is simply not enough time to do it any other way. The CROPing dynamic is alive and well and an important one to tap into for marketers.

I am the general manager of a radio group. Our station is a strong female-skewing station. I read your article in *BRAND-WEEK*. It was useful and inspiring. Do you have additional articles, books, etc. that you would recommend?

Businesses are seeking resources to help them more effectively reach women.

Just as female consumers are CROPing, businesses and brands are seeking shortcuts to credible and useful information. Business people face challenges similar to those encountered by female consumers—so much to do and so little time. I have included a bibliography and a list of resources at the end of this book that can help marketers do some of their own CROPing when it comes to marketing to women.

One fact stands out. In these times of busy lives and a complicated, fiercely competitive marketplace, a good friend is even more effective than a good ad, in-store display, or Web site in influencing a woman's purchasing decisions.

M^2 Must-Dos

✓ Remember that before women shop, they CROP, or seek CRedible OPinions, as a shortcut to purchases.

✓ Give friends and family something to talk about by earning editorial coverage in both local and national media.

✓ Inform and engage influential experts and women before your general audience.

✓ Assist your female consumer by making her product research easier.

✓ Remember that "friends and family" can be in-person or online. Ensure that you are connecting with key online influencers like blogs and social networking sites as they provide the filters for many brands and branded sites.

✓ Engage online search engines as the front line to point consumers in your direction.

Chapter Eight

The Keys to Connecting with Multi-Minding Women

"Special K is a real 'partner' in my shape management," says Lisa. "I feel like we are really in it together, even though my life is crazy and I don't always eat the way I want to."

What an interesting comment. Think about it: this woman views a brand as a "partner," something that helps her *and* she actually blames *herself*, not the brand, when she does not achieve a perfect outcome. Wow. What is going on here? It looks like the brand is so connected and intertwined with the consumer that there is a real relationship, complete with give and take.

How many brands or businesses can claim that level of connectivity? Based on my personal experiences and what I have seen and read, not enough. A great deal of what you read in the advertising trades—and a good deal of what I have heard in client meetings—includes words like "interrupt," "intercept," "breakthrough," and "capture," and much less often talks about "connecting." Connectivity has been a missing link in the land of marketing to women. As the multi-minding phenomenon grows, connectivity will take on increasing importance.

CONNECT THE DOTS FOR MULTI-MINDING WOMEN

You can compare marketing connectivity to any business or personal relationship that you care about in real life. If you want it to be successful, the relationship requires a thoughtful introduction, relevant messages, engagement, and consistency. Those same concepts apply to marketing to multi-minding women.

Let's dig a bit deeper into what connectivity means. Research conducted by the Ketchum Global Research Network revealed the following key findings among female consumers (see table 8.1). To make a long story short, women are busier on average than men or the general population. They are jugglers, physically and mentally, trying to handle

Table 8.1   Women Are More Likely to Agree That ...

Question: On a scale of 1 to 5, where 1 is 'completely disagree' and 5 is 'completely agree,' how would you rate this statement? Percent totals are summary of the top two choices.

	Total Public	Men 25–54	Women 25–54
I juggle a lot of tasks.	68%	67%	81%
I wish there were more hours in the day to get things done.	65%	66%	76%
There are many things competing for my attention at the same time.	61%	60%	74%
I spend more time thinking about other's needs than my own.	59%	50%	74%
I juggle a lot of thoughts.	63%	63%	72%
In the course of two minutes, I have multiple thoughts running through my mind.	58%	54%	68%
I have little time for commercial messages.	54%	50%	62%
I constantly feel pulled in different directions.	45%	42%	61%
I wish I had more time during the day to think.	50%	50%	59%
I have to read or hear something more than once because I am often distracted or interrupted.	31%	26%	39%

Source: Ketchum Global Research Network, Women 25 to 54 Launch Study, 2005.

a great deal of information and activity in a short amount of time. These women can give only short amounts of time to each activity and, increasingly, they choose not to pay attention to commercial messages as a way to filter information and save time. Women also think about others in their lives more than they think about their own needs.

These findings and their implications provide the keys to understanding "connectivity." Lack of time, competition for share of mind, busy schedules, and focus on others are challenges that require marketers to take a "new and improved" approach to reaching their female consumers. Defining an approach that achieves connectivity requires solutions to the four challenges revealed in the research:

- What will help them save time?
- How can I introduce my brand or service—quickly?
- How can I engage in their busy schedules?
- How can I stay on their minds when they are thinking about others' needs and their own?

A BETTER WAY

While working at Ketchum, I was the lead architect in developing a process that addressed those very questions. We call the process "Women 25 to 54, A Better Way to Reach Female Consumers." Taking into consideration the proprietary research developed by Ketchum, as well as other studies on similar topics, we created a four-phased process that helps marketers understand how to better reach multi-minding women today.

I will go into the details of the process and examples in chapters 9 through 13, with a chapter devoted to each of the four phases. The cornerstone concepts are Credibility, Quick-Connect Messaging, E-surround Programming, and Consistent Confirmation. Let's briefly talk about each of these cornerstones and see how they play out in real life.

Credibility is a good foundation for any marketing or communications program aimed at women. It takes time to build and just a moment to lose, and it now exists on two levels—brand and company. Women need to feel that the brand itself is credible, because it delivers on its promises, has a good reputation, and can be trusted. In addition, the company is now being held to those same standards.

One of the secrets to building and sustaining brand credibility is having the information about the brand delivered by credible sources. Who does your female consumer trust and can you reach consumers through that trusted source? You'd think there would be as many credible sources as there are product categories, but interestingly, women deem the same sources credible when it comes to making purchases in a variety of product categories.

Information from family and friends tops women's lists across all categories with 9 in 10, or 91 percent, saying these sources provide "very" or "somewhat" credible information, according to recent research.[1] Get the family and friends of your target audience talking, and you have a direct route to credibility. Hence, the current buzz about word-of-mouth marketing—a communications vehicle that will be part of every marketer's toolkit in coming years.

After family and friends, a number of studies cite experts as a very credible source of information for female consumers. Keep in mind that experts will vary, depending on the product or service. A food product that is trying to communicate nutrition would be well served to engage registered dietitians from the American Dietetic Association, while a paint company may look to a personality from HGTV.

Remember, with credibility at stake, your expert should really believe in and use your product. I also think it helps tremendously when your expert is a reflection of your target audience. Trying to reach moms with small children about nutrition? Create relationships with registered dietitians who are also moms with small children and see value in using your product. They not only are experts in their field, but also can relate to the real life of your female consumer.

FINDING A GOOD CAUSE

Credibility at a company level is increasingly on the radar screen of the average female consumer. One of the ways I have seen companies or brands add to their credibility is through cause marketing—aligning with a nonprofit cause or societal issue that they help in some way. Wikipedia defines cause marketing as "a type of marketing involving the cooperative efforts of a for-profit business and a nonprofit organization for mutual benefit."[2]

American Express is generally credited with creating the term "cause marketing," thanks to its Statue of Liberty Restoration project in 1983.[3] Cause marketing is being embraced by a growing number of American companies with $1.1 billion spent in 2005, $1.34 billion in 2006, and even more predicted for coming years.[4]

The pioneer in the field of cause branding, Cone Inc., has partnered with leading organizations and companies to create and implement some of the nation's most effective cause initiatives, including the Avon Breast Cancer Crusade, the PNC Grow Up Great campaign, and ConAgra's Feeding Children Better effort. According to the 2007 Cone Cause Evolution Survey, business practices are now an additional purchasing influence for about one-third of American shoppers. And, a whopping 85 percent of Americans say they would switch to another company's products or services if a problem with business practices was uncovered.[5] Clearly, credibility at the brand and company levels has an impact on consumers and sales.

I talked with Carol L. Cone, founder and chief executive of Cone, about cause marketing and building credibility with female consumers. She shared several insightful points. For instance, it is critical to link with female consumers on a values-based issue.

"It's not just about features and benefits. Companies need a values orientation that is about doing something greater than making money," Cone points out. "The parent company sets the tone for the brands and then the brands should deliver on those values, too."

The research done by Cone's company and others supports consumers' desire to consider corporate and brand reputation when making a purchase. Cause is no longer a "nice to do" effort; it's a "have to do" responsibility, according to the Americans surveyed in the 2007 Cause Evolution Survey.[6] Perhaps most interesting, the research revealed that this stance is even more prominent with women than with men. According to the 2007 survey, 84 percent of women say they consider a company's commitment to social issues when deciding what to buy or where to shop, compared with 75 percent of men.[7] Given that this trend has been consistently growing over time, cause connectivity is fast becoming an expectation, especially among women.

Combine that expectation with women being relationship-oriented and you will find that cause efforts cannot be transient if they are to be effective.

"Cause branding—the true, real deep, authentic causes—is executed over time. Great cause branding is like great architecture," Cone notes.

It requires extensive planning, a footprint that can withstand the tests of time, and executing the plans with innovation and credibility. The implementation is critical because that's where you develop the linkages to engage. We call it the spectrum of engagement.

Cone points out Avon's connections to breast cancer and PNC's Grow Up Great early education program as two examples of both innovation and commitment over time.

"In 1992, Avon's then-CEO wanted another meaningful way to connect with his female consumers," Cone recalls. "Avon's breast cancer initiatives have thrived through two other CEOs and the efforts are bigger and better than ever today."

The CEO connection is important to note. In Cone's experiences, "the really impactful, well-funded, long-term, consistent cause programs are driven by the c-suite. It's about corporate strategy, not a quick notion to support a worthy cause." She describes the CEOs who are committing to cause activities as "the early adopters of cause who 'get it.'" These companies and brands are poised to forge ahead of their competitors now and in the future in the minds of female consumers, who clearly value the efforts and are willing to put their money where their hearts are.

Based on the research in the Cone Cause Evolution Study and the 2006 Cone Millennial Cause Study, cause-related activity will continue to grow. With 87 percent of Americans and 89 percent of millennials (Americans 13 to 25 years old) saying they are "likely" or "very likely" to switch from one brand to another (price and quality being equal), if the second brand is associated with a good cause.[8] Cone predicts that cause initiatives will become de rigueur in the next decade.

Women seem to be driving the decision to switch to brands that are associated with a good cause. If you break down that 87 percent of

Americans who are likely to switch, 89 percent of women versus 85 percent of men held that belief. With millennials, the driving force with women is even more striking. Of the 89 percent of millennials who would switch, 92 percent of females hold that opinion, compared with 85 percent of males.[9]

"Cause can apply to any company, business, or brand," Cone emphasizes.

> What you need, and what consumers want, is content, which will make it harder and harder for advertising to address with so many micro-audiences. Content comes from human stories and from a cause, and any brand or business can have those. All of the causes are not taken. Any company or brand, large or small, can own a cause that they can impact.

WHAT OTHERS SAY IS MORE CREDIBLE THAN WHAT YOU SAY ABOUT YOURSELF

Studies show that editorial media, both national and local including print, online, television, and radio, rank in the top 10 most credible sources of information.[10] Editorial media, or earned media, is the news and related coverage found in newspapers and magazines, on Web sites, and on television and radio. It is not advertising, but rather part of the "news." It is considered credible expressly because it is not paid commercial messaging. Some good examples include new product reviews for cosmetics in *InStyle* magazine, food products specified in recipes on the Food Network, or the holy grail of earned media—one of Oprah's picks for her annual "Favorite Things" show.

Other sources that rank high on the credibility list for women are consumer opinion and rating Web sites and shopping Web sites that include consumer reviews. I think of these sites as a virtual extension of family and friends and a place where women can gather many opinions and recommendations in an instant. Table 7.1 details the most credible sources of information for the Women 25 to 54 category.

BE QUICK ABOUT IT

Now that we have built a strong foundation for our marketing regarding credibility, we need to connect with our consumers through messages that resonate ... and fast. Keep in mind that time is at a premium for our consumer and that she has little time for commercial messages. Long-form and complicated messages will be deflected by these women. That is why the second cornerstone in the Women 25 to 54 approach implores that the bite-size messages be repeatable across any communications medium.

Think "weight-management partner," not "it will help you lose those unsightly extra pounds in just one month with meals that are prepared and delivered to your door for just pennies a day." Try using "you can make nutritious, home-cooked meals," rather than "studies over the years have shown that canned fruits and vegetables are proven to be as nutritious as frozen and fresh when prepared for the table." Consider "we believe in girls," as opposed to a dizzying parade of ongoing personalities, clothes, and upgrades to a Barbie doll. Try one-click buying, similar to what is available on Amazon.com, instead of requiring consumers to type those tedious contact details every time they visit your Web site.

Think about how you can save your female consumer time and create a message that can be communicated to her via any and all of your communications efforts. Involving your consumer in message creation and testing will ensure that your message is the best one.

I should add an important caveat about Quick-Connect Messaging. Multi-tasking and multi-minding are driving women to demand messages that are relevant and quickly communicated. These same women do, however, often want and need to research their product purchases before buying. Table 8.2 shows how likely women are to do research for a sampling of product categories.

Even with categories like food and consumer-packaged goods, which are relatively inexpensive items, women are likely to do some research before buying. Moreover, with categories like consumer electronics, where items tend to be relatively expensive, the vast majority of female consumers do some or a lot of research.

Women want to make informed decisions on large purchases, though smaller ones can be made on impulse. Mothers, more than women without children, say they rarely make impulsive purchases (37 percent versus 31 percent, respectively), but nonmothers are more likely than mothers to do research before making big purchases (76 percent versus 70 percent, respectively).[11]

With women conducting research before making purchasing decisions, it is critical to provide tools to enable that research. Web sites are

Table 8.2   Women Do Research Before Shopping

	A Little/ No Research	Some/A Lot of Research
Consumer Packaged Goods	45%	55%
Food	53%	47%
Consumer Electronics	18%	82%

Source: Ketchum Global Research Network, Women 25 to 54 Study, 2006.

one of the most common, cost-effective, and frequently accessed vehicles for information gathering. Depending on the needs of your audience and the complexity of your product or service, it also may be useful to include brochures, seminars, and the input of experts that women may consult.

A DAY IN THE LIFE OF A MARKETING MESSAGE

Our multi-minding consumer is busier than ever before, and it is likely that this phenomenon will not be reversed. While Janet may be watching the *Today* show at 7:30 in the morning, she also is packing school lunches for her two kids, making coffee for herself, chatting with her husband about tomorrow's schedule, scanning the local newspaper, and thinking about some research she needs to do for a meeting later in the afternoon.

Given that common scenario, it is understandable and likely that she will not fully absorb an article about an environmentally friendly residential flooring product called Marmoleum that was featured in the newspaper that morning. Even though this consumer wants to make her home more "green," she just does not have the time right now to find out more.

When Janet hops in the car, she turns on the radio, which she then turns down so she can talk with the kids about plans for the weekend. Once the kids are at school, she returns home and flips on the television to catch a few minutes of *The View*, which Janet likes because of the hosts' candid views. That day, the show is devoted to green products for the home and Marmoleum Click, a do-it-yourself version of Marmoleum, is featured. Janet needs to start her work day, so she cannot listen to the whole segment, but she makes a mental note to find out more.

Later that week, Janet visits some of her favorite Web sites—the ones that provide quick, easy, and simple tips for managing the chaos of family and home. She notices an article by a leading expert on consumer green products. Marmoleum is one of the products mentioned. A few weeks later, she takes her son to baseball practice and flips through a favorite magazine hunting for recipe ideas. How about that— Marmoleum is cited as one of the best products when remodeling or building a home that will be healthy for your family. Janet takes note that Marmoleum is aligned with the World Wildlife Federation, a cause she and her family support.

Janet's time is clearly at a premium. She is *always* making her time do double duty. Therefore, the marketing that will succeed with this woman is the marketing that lives everywhere she is living—at home, in the car, at work, and at leisure. In this case, the messages that the Marmoleum floor-covering product is delivering succeed in surrounding Janet. The bite-size messages also must be repeatable, so she can quickly grasp them and associate them back to the product, no matter when or where she experiences them.

FROM B-TO-B TO B-TO-C

I spoke with Denis Darragh, general manager of Forbo Flooring Systems/North America and Asia. Forbo is the company that makes Marmoleum, which has been marketed for commercial use for decades to architects and designers. Now that the product is available in a do-it-yourself version, called Marmoleum Click, the business-to-business marketing has evolved to include consumer marketing. Darragh has learned a great deal based on his experiences in marketing Marmoleum to women today. He stresses,

> Research tells us that the top three reasons consumers choose Marmoleum are color and design, having a healthy home environment, and the fact that it is a sustainable product. But in my mind, there is an ever more important, fundamental cornerstone when you are marketing to women. There must be a trust relationship, almost to the corporate level. Women want to be able to trust what and who is behind a product.

That insight dovetails with Carol Cone's comments earlier in this chapter. It is the combined credibility of the brand and its parent company that drives deep trust.

Darragh goes on to comment on how credibility is delivered. "Women have individuals or peer groups that validate purchase considerations. What a manufacturer says is not perceived nearly as credibly as what an objective peer or expert says." Darragh's experiences show that women are the most well-informed consumers and they pursue information to the fullest extent. The Ketchum research supports Darragh's theory that women conduct considerable research before they make a purchase.

"What will make it easier for women when it comes to sustainable products like ours is a seal of approval—a label or shortcut that vouches for credibility," notes Darragh. "The key is making the standard itself be credible through a transparent development process and third-party auditing." A good and tangible example of a seal of approval in the building product category is SMaRT Certified, a program of the Institute for Market Transformation to Sustainability (MTS), which considers the product's complete lifecycle.

Such a seal of approval helps women save time, an extremely important factor for multi-minding women. Darragh stresses that "being respectful of a woman's decision-making process" is another critical factor. "Let women choose to decide to buy rather than trying to close a sale." This insight can be particularly helpful to companies that traditionally have operated in the business-to-business arena and are branching out to market directly to female consumers.

It is imperative that your marketing live in all of the dimensions and areas of your multi-minding consumers' lives. They may not be able to fully absorb any one message, but the cumulative effort is needed to have her see your product as part of her life.

The Dove Campaign for Real Beauty has done an outstanding job of surrounding its female consumers with relevant messages. An integrated campaign of television and print advertising, outdoor billboards, far-reaching editorial coverage in women's magazines, a fresh and inviting Web site, viral online videos, a cause-marketing component, and a call-to-action for consumers made it a campaign you literally could not miss.

KEEP IT GOING

The final cornerstone for a better way to reach female consumers is something that sounds so simple, but it is usually the first thing cut from the marketing budget—Consistent Confirmation. Just like in real life, relationships are not built overnight. It takes time and consistent effort. When planning a marketing campaign, what I often see companies do is quite different from what I just described.

A good deal of any marketing spending is put behind "new" or "new and improved" products. A launch for a new product typically commands the lion's share of the budget. Time, effort, and money are focused on getting the product out to the marketplace with a great deal of fanfare. After that big launch, many brands and companies are out of budget, so they do nothing, or relatively little, to sustain the relationship with the consumer.

Questions Every Marketer or Business Owner Should Ask

- What is my brand or business doing that will help women save time or make their time do double duty?

- Is my brand or business engaged with a relevant cause that reflects the essence of the business and relevancy to my female consumers?

- Am I using multiple communications channels to communicate my message?

- Am I using brief messages that quickly will connect with my female consumers and providing tools, such as a Web site, that will allow consumers to do research and explore details?

When I present this concept to major marketers, they almost always laugh—that laugh of recognition that I have hit on an uncomfortable truth. Then they agree, because that is what happens. The planning and support to continue the effort has either been seen as not needed or has been cut from the budget.

When marketing to female consumers, though, this sustainability, or Consistent Confirmation as I call it, is critical. Remember credibility? Well, a big flash in the pan may drive initial interest, but credibility builds over time, especially with women who are relationship oriented.

Now you might ask, "Wait a minute ... you keep stressing that the multi-minding female consumer does not have time. How could she want a relationship?" Doesn't that take her precious time? Indeed, it does and that is why Consistent Confirmation is very much woven into her life and is not considered to be time-consuming or invasive. Ideally, this consistency should succeed in reaffirming her purchasing decisions and enable her to be an ambassador for your brand or business.

JUST-IN-TIME DELIVERY

I have another great example. An organization called the Canned Food Alliance (CFA) educates women about the nutritional benefits of canned foods. The CFA uses distilled, relevant messages and surrounds its audience with information from experts, editorial media, and a word-of-mouth program. The Consistent Confirmation part of the communications effort is brilliant in its relevance and timing. Once a week at 3:00 PM, an e-mail is sent to registered users of its Web site, Mealtime. org. The e-mail provides quick, healthy, and tasty recipes for dinner that night, and they are delivered right as the audience is starting to think about what's for dinner.

That is a perfect example of bite-size, relevant information delivered at an optimal time by a trusted source, and it is a cost-effective communications vehicle. That is a Consistent Confirmation home run.

Web sites provide an ideal way to achieve consistent and cost-effective confirmation. Postpurchase surveys, product seedings (providing new products in advance to a group of loyal users), user groups, and ongoing consumer panels are all methods to achieve Consistent Confirmation.

As Cone notes, "Women are the keepers of relationships, whether personal, business or community. Companies and brands must be in a relationship with this consumer to succeed over time."

M^2 Must-Dos

✓ Link to female consumers via a values-based idea that extends beyond just features and benefits.

✓ Implement ongoing cause-related efforts that are authentically aligned with your company or brand.

✓ Saturate the audience with communications during key "moments in time" for your product or service.

✓ Serve as a real partner and ongoing resource for her in between and after purchase by proactively offering information, tips, and resources.

✓ Provide a 24/7 forum for women to discuss topics related to your product or business.

Chapter Nine

The Better Way: A New Approach to Reach Female Consumers

"There has to be a better way," I thought as I talked with marketers and female consumers. Neither side is getting what it wants with the current state of marketing. Marketers of all types, who now want to reach the lucrative female consumer marketplace, are being met with skepticism. Meanwhile, women, who are the primary purchasers of most goods and services, feel ignored or insulted by marketing efforts.

BRANDWEEK magazine notes, "Consumers are winning the arms race against advertisers. They have more tools at their disposal now and are so jaded that some won't even trust a recommendation of a friend for fear that they've been gulled by a word-of-mouth campaign."[1]

That "better way," as I have alluded to throughout the book, is not a single, magic bullet. Rather, it *is* a holistic approach that resonates with women—a blueprint, if you will, for a better way to reach female consumers. Why is such a comprehensive approach needed to successfully reach female consumers?

"It all boils down to one fundamental difference," notes Marti Barletta, well-known author and president of the Trendsight Group. "Men look for a good solution and women look for a perfect answer." Barletta explains that women think about things more contextually and put together a more comprehensive picture; hence, the need for a holistic approach.

A MARKETER'S WORK IS NEVER DONE

As with any successful relationship, it is a journey, not a destination. It is not something that you can check off your activity list for the day and say "done!" It is, however, worth the effort. To lag behind and do less with today's powerful, techno-savvy, multi-minding female consumer eventually will erode your bottom line.

With work, home, and family responsibilities, today's woman has become busier than ever and harder than ever for marketers to reach. At any one moment, she is thinking about choices related to career, household, spousal, motherhood, and personal responsibilities. Consequently, these women have moved from multi-tasking to a new level of multi-minding.

As you recall from previous chapters, multi-minding is the perpetual state of mind for today's typical 25- to 54-year-old woman, who constantly deals with the multiple dimensions of her life, whether she is sorting out a work project, helping with a child's school project, or even relaxing by watching a television show. She is abuzz with the many facets of her life. As a result, she has little time for commercial messages.

Marketers can tap into women's complex multi-minding state of mind. As a *BusinessWeek* online article on the topic states, "Whether their efforts involve retraining sales staff or redesigning products, companies that pay attention to the female consumer could hit the mother lode."[2]

THE KEY CORNERSTONES TO REACH WOMEN

After talking personally with many female consumers and marketers, conducting research, reviewing media coverage, and keeping an eye on trends, I have concluded that successful marketing to women hinges on four critical cornerstones: Credibility, Quick-Connect Messaging, E-surround Programming, and Consistent Confirmation.

The work that my team and I at Ketchum have done led to a four-phase communications program that fulfills an unmet need in the marketplace to reach today's super-consumer, the 25- to 54-year-old woman. This approach, called "Women 25 to 54," delivers credible messaging that quickly and completely connects to this critical consumer audience.

The four-phase foundation of Women 25 to 54 identifies, creates, disseminates, and reinforces credible messaging for today's multi-minding women:

- **"What Really Matters" Credibility Index**. In the first phase, a process concisely and accurately identifies the messages and messengers that will quickly and credibly resonate with multi-minding women.
- **Quick-Connect Messaging.** The second phase creates "bite-size," repeatable messaging for women by employing Ketchum's Quick-Connect Message Map.
- **E-surround Programming.** For the third phase, a process determines the right mix of editors, experts, equals, and entertainment marketing outlets to target communications containing messages that blend with women's lifestyles and surround them with credible information.

- **Consistent Confirmation.** In the final phase, post-program activities reinforce purchasing decisions and drive word-of-mouth endorsements.

To bring these concepts to life, I thought it would be helpful to show you a real-life example of how one of my clients, the Canned Food Alliance (CFA), engaged the approach. In addition, an interview with Hedy Lukas, vice president of integrated marketing at Kimberly-Clark Corp., sheds light on how Credibility, Quick-Connect Messaging, E-surround Programming, and Consistent Confirmation are being used to market some of the company's biggest brands, like Kleenex facial tissue, Huggies disposable diapers, and VIVA paper towels, to women.

THE CASE OF THE CANNED FOOD ALLIANCE

Let's take a look at the marketing-to-women work that has been done by the CFA. A decade ago, sales of canned foods were predicted to decline sharply. Research conducted for the CFA showed that one of the major reasons for the decline was a perception by women, the primary purchasers of canned foods, that canned foods were not nutritious. Women still buy canned products and they are found in nearly every U.S. household in some form because of a positive perception of the products' convenience. The perception about nutritional value, however, was identified as a primary obstacle to increased purchases.

CFA executive director Rich Tavoletti recalls the situation. "The steel industry was concerned that domestic shipments of steel, steel that goes into making cans for food, were projected to decline. We started asking ourselves what could be done to impact the end market."

The steel industry had a vision and commissioned consumer research that showed perception was generally negative for canned foods, especially when it came to taste and nutrition.

"Armed with that research, the steel industry went to its customers, the can makers, and their customers, the food processors, which began a partnership that is still alive today," says Tavoletti.

The CFA, a consortium of major food processors, can makers, and steel makers, was formed. The organization serves as a resource for information on the nutritional value, contemporary appeal, and versatility of canned foods. I congratulate the CFA and its members because they have committed to this effort, no doubt a long-term proposition, for nearly 10 years. Over time, the CFA has engaged women in a comprehensive communications effort using a combination of nutrition research, public relations, spokesperson publicity and endorsement, trade show participation, retail merchandising, online marketing and partnerships, advertising, and sales promotions.

A FOUNDATION OF RESEARCH

"The benchmark research conducted by the steel industry served as both a rallying cry for the partnership and a benchmark for our efforts over time," Tavoletti says. "The partners remain committed because we can show progress over time in successfully reaching the consumers who are the primary purchasers of canned foods: women with children.

"We started the program by communicating to women through both advertising and public relations," he adds. "Over time, our budget became leaner and we saw positive results with public relations, so we invested our budget there."

I think the CFA was ahead of its time in terms of communications strategy. The CFA transitioned out of advertising due to cost, but the credibility it delivered through public relations is absolutely key to changing deep-seated perceptions, which is the case with canned foods.

Research has shown that, when forming perceptions for food and nutrition, women turn to editorial media (nonadvertising coverage), experts (dietitians and chefs), equals (family and friends), and even to some entertainment sources (like the Food Network). As we defined credibility for the CFA, we knew we must be communicating through those four credible sources—editorial media, experts, equals, and entertainment. Just a quick word on editorial media or nonpaid media. It is not advertising; it is the content—article or story—in a media outlet. Inclusion in editorial content is typically achieved through public relations and is deemed by consumers to be more credible, on average, than advertising. The CFA has been successful in generating editorial coverage in magazines, newspapers, on television, radio, and online for its nutrition and convenience messages.

MULTIPLE MESSENGERS

"Those who directly represent an organization, like the CFA, could be seen to have biased viewpoints, so influencers and spokespeople are key," says Tavoletti.

We have research that proves the nutritional value of canned foods, and we know that women turn to certain credible sources of information when it comes to nutrition. Therefore, we put that research into the hands of influencers and spokespeople. With the consumers' best interests in mind, those credible sources helped deliver messages that could seem less credible coming from our partners.

Women trust relevant experts and tapping experts lends credibility to marketing campaigns. To deliver its messages, the CFA has engaged spokespeople, including celebrity chefs, culinary experts, and nutrition experts. Food Network star Tyler Florence and the quintessential chef, Jacques Pepin, as well as nutrition researchers and well-known registered dieticians, have served as messengers for the CFA. Several years ago, the CFA even sponsored a PBS show, called *Fast Food My Way*, that starred Pepin. This stable of spokespeople, which changes based on trends and insights, has driven credibility and news for the CFA and its recipe Web site. Importantly, the CFA has added "mom" to its criteria for spokespeople in the past few years. These people carry expert credentials in the nutrition or culinary world, and they also are moms.

"We've taken a variety of directions over the years with spokespeople," Tavoletti notes.

> Celebrity chefs and culinary experts, at the top of their game when it comes to flavor, have helped carry messages about taste and using canned foods in really good-tasting recipes. We have found that it's helpful to leverage expert credentials and to have our expert be a mom, too, so she can speak as a mom to other moms.

MESSAGING THAT IS MULTI-MINDING-FRIENDLY

Messages that quickly connect were the next challenge. One of the advantages that the CFA has is that the messages are unbranded, meaning they are applied to an entire category of products, not just specific brands. Tavoletti believes the unbranded voice of the CFA provides credibility in the eyes of female consumers. He stressed that consumers and the CFA member companies place high value on the nonbranded nature of the program.

Do not underestimate the value of participating in nonbranded communications. It is a highly credible supplement to the more common branded marketing that most businesses and brands undertake. Cynical, time-pressed female consumers are interested in what most benefits them, not in what benefits a marketer most. Nonbranded initiatives are seen as much less commercial and, therefore, much more credible.

Research and experience tell us that women do not have a lot of time to absorb the information. Offering shorter chunks of information for women to digest will help them cut through the clutter. The CFA's messages were well-founded, but wordy. We needed to distill the messages to something that would resonate with the busy mom we were trying to reach. Simply "nutritious" was used instead of the former "canned foods are as nutritious as their fresh and frozen counterparts when prepared for the table." Likewise, just the Web site name, "Mealtime.org," replaced "visit the Canned Food Alliance's Web site, Mealtime.org, for recipes and nutrition information."

No matter who the messenger and no matter what the length of the article or story, those simple and relevant messages could always be communicated. The Mealtime.org message served as the call to action that led women to recipes, nutrition information, and the mealtime online community. The Web site provides rich and robust information about nutrition, answers frequently asked questions, and offers hundreds of simple and nutritious recipes.

More work is being done to "relevate" the messages further to meet the core needs and anxieties of many busy moms for whom dinner time can be stressful. "We plan to evolve the CFA messages to focus on enhancing perceptions, not just battling negatives," vows Tavoletti.

HOLISTIC IS REALISTIC

Women are certainly multi-minding, and so your marketing messages are likely to be missed if they exist in just one channel. In the case of the CFA, the messages have been used in "E-surround Programming," or 360-degree touch point communications programming to the four credible sources of information—editorial media, experts, equals (including other consumers), and entertainment. While the elements are tweaked each year, here is a sample of the comprehensive marketing program that has been implemented in past years.

"We can't afford to cover all bases with our budget," says Tavoletti, "but we know we have to be in a number of key places to credibly reach our audience of moms, including the editorial media, nutrition influencers, and online."

ACTIONS SPEAK LOUDER THAN WORDS

Finally, one of the easiest, but most often forgotten, elements to the holistic Women 25 to 54 approach is Consistent Confirmation, or making the program thrive long after the initial launch. When I talk to many brand managers about this topic, they admit that this type of activity is usually an afterthought, if a thought at all. Most of the funding seems to go to the launch or big events, and then the flow of information stops.

If women want ongoing relationships, stopping the flow of information is certainly counterproductive. This consistency does not have to be expensive or expansive. One of the ways the CFA achieves Consistent Confirmation is through dinnertime e-mails that are sent to its database of Web site users. Since many women do not start thinking about what they will put on the table for dinner until about 3:00 PM, CFA's dinnertime e-mails provide recipes at the right time of the day to solve that dinner dilemma.

This well-timed, relatively inexpensive, and consistent marketing tool enables the CFA to be a solution and drives consumers to product trial and purchase via the recipes. It is a great example of Consistent Confirmation.

"If you want to make it onto a woman's radar screen, provide quality information on your Web site," notes Holly Buchanan, who writes a blog called Marketing to Women Online.[3]

IT'S WORKING!

These collective efforts have resulted in key message delivery in just about every media outlet that reaches women, including *USA Today*, the *Today* show, *Better Homes and Gardens*, *American Baby*, *iVillage*, and *Health* magazine, to name just a few. Nearly 1 million women a year visit the organization's unbranded Web site, Mealtime.org, to access and rate recipes. Thousands of influencers, including dieticians and health professionals, have been reached via an ongoing influencer relationship-management effort.

The initiative is designed to educate women ages 25 to 45 with children about the convenience, versatility, and nutritional value of canned food. And, it's working. General market research indicates that perceptions regarding nutrition have improved over time. Specific research that measures the campaign elements shows that targeted women, as well as key influencers like dieticians and influential media, have changed their perceptions over time.

"The CFA measures progress toward its key goals by measuring consumer perceptions," Tavoletti explains. "We also look at tactical measures like media impressions, Web site visitors, and cost per thousand. Given the scope of our program, we cannot reach everyone, so we look at a general population survey in conjunction with the opinions of the moms and influencers who we know we've reached."

Tavoletti and the CFA are right on trend as they look to measure the perceptions and behaviors of their specific target audience and not the general population. Many marketers are turning away from mass communications as costs increase and consumer impact decreases. Through technology and digital communications, it is becoming even more possible to reach many women in much more targeted, credible, and effective ways.

What is really exciting and impressive is that a recent pilot campaign, which included in-home parties and online promotions, resulted not only in drastically improved perceptions, but also in increased purchase intent. Specifically, 61 percent of those women who participated in the in-home events said their perceptions improved and 58 percent of attendees reported an increase in the likelihood to buy canned foods—all as a result of participating in the CFA's program. The program, which has already won an industry award from the Public Relations Society of America, is being used by members as a testing ground for future marketing activities for individual brands.

NOT A CANNED APPROACH TO THE FUTURE

The program elements have evolved and changed over time, but the CFA's delivery of Credibility, Quick-Connect Messaging, E-surround Programming, and Consistent Confirmation has remained. Based on this robust and evolving program, I asked Tavoletti what one thing he would recommend to marketers as they look to engage multi-minding women. I was impressed by his answer and how consistent it was with what Leslie Morgan Steiner, author of *Mommy Wars* (2006), said earlier in the book.

He recommends, "Women, and especially moms, are strapped for time. Don't make them feel guilty. Be a help. Make life easier." For example, simplify a stressful dinner time by helping them put a meal on the table for their family. Offer solutions and be part of the solution. In the future, Tavoletti predicts more online activity in the marketing-to-women space and for the CFA.

"Moms tell us they want to share thoughts, ideas, and challenges, and online venues are great ways to do just that," he says.

BETTER WAYS TO REACH WOMEN EMERGING ACROSS INDUSTRY

The CFA is forging new and better ways to reach its audience of moms. Other organizations, companies, and brands are exploring, testing, and implementing various methods for reaching women in better ways—holistic ways—that really connect. Kimberly-Clark Corp. is one such company. I spoke with Hedy Lukas, vice president of integrated marketing at Kimberly-Clark, whose team of marketers is doing interesting things in the marketing-to-women space.

"In the past, we used to focus on giving women incentives, like coupons or samples, to drive purchase. It was a one-way dialogue about the brand that worked for a long time," explains Lukas. "Now, we are trying to find ways to connect with women, not through incentives, but through an emotional connection that enables a two-way dialogue. Consumers are human beings and human beings connect through meaningful ways. Brands are catching on to that concept."

A good example of Lukas' approach is Huggies, Kimberly-Clark's disposable diaper brand.

"We used to provide mothers of newborns with coupons. It was a transactionally based relationship and we sold a lot of diapers, but today, consumers' needs and demands are evolving along with technology," says Lukas.

Now, we engage women when they are first pregnant via our Huggies Baby Network. That Web site allows expectant mothers to access a wealth of helpful information and connect with other expectant mothers at a time in their lives when information and connection are extremely important. Huggies is part of a solution for the expectant mother, even though these consumers are not yet in the market for diapers.

Another Kimberly-Clark brand, Scott, has homed in on an emotional connector with its female audience. Lukas says that research shows Scott Tissue's core consumers are value-conscious and proud of their common-sense approach to buying products.

"Our Scott Common Sense Community is visited by thousands of consumers who share a common bond," she says. "There is no immediate transactional value to the Scott brand, but we are taking a longer-term view of building relationships, and believe those relationships will engender a long-term following."

In both the Huggies and Scott examples, the brands have succeeded in identifying the core audience and relevant connection points. They are not trying to be all things to all people. The brands realize their success rests in the hands of their core consumers and have taken the time to understand what matters to those women. In each case, it is different—as it will be with your brand or business.

Many experts in this book have cited building relationships as a key to marketing successfully to women now and in the future. Lukas offers some thoughts and tips on how it can be done. For example, she points out that technology makes relationship-building personal and affordable.

"The interaction that technology enables just wasn't possible in the past," she says. "Direct mail and other personalizable vehicles were cost-prohibitive for us."

The right mind-set is an important consideration, as well. "In the past, brands saw their role as selling things," adds Lukas. "Today, more and more brands realize they can be and should be connectors that will create a more robust and loyal following. The commercial benefit will stem from a successful relationship."

Research shows how important credibility is in marketing to female consumers. Women have a keen ability to smell a rat or discern when something just does not seem believable, even when they cannot see direct evidence. Chapter 7 on credibility delves into how women view credibility and how it can be achieved.

Lukas offers her point of view on credibility and I think it represents a sound approach.

"Be true to yourself. Be true to your brand. Be genuine," she suggests. Like many ideas in this book, that advice is easier said than done and there is no single, magic-bullet answer.

"If the goal is a sustained relationship, you must be honest with your consumers." You can't create a relationship solely on a transaction.

Women can see through it and will be turned off. Don't overstep your role," advises Lukas. "Women don't want a disposable diaper or a paper towel to be their best friend, but there are places in their lives where they will invite and welcome a genuine connection."

The Kleenex "Let It Out" campaign is a good example of a brand that did just that.

"Kleenex found a positioning, 'let it out,' that celebrated emotional expression. The campaign showed it was OK to cry, OK to be emotional, OK to express those emotions, and Kleenex is there for you any time you need to let it out," says Lukas. "Consumers loved the campaign because emotional expression is relevant to them and placing the Kleenex brand as their friend in those circumstances was valid and welcome."

"CHOICEFUL" COMMUNICATIONS AND CHANNELS

Kimberly-Clark is also breaking ground in its philosophy for selecting the channels through which it will reach women. While many companies are talking about breaking away from mass communications and its mainstay, the 30-second television spot, few have acted on the notion.

"We are beginning our marketing planning as a channel-neutral process, meaning we are not making assumptions that mass advertising will drive marketing as we may have in the past," Lukas explains. "After that, we become channel-selective. We can't afford to be everywhere and consumers don't want to be barraged with information from everywhere, so we make 'choiceful' decisions based on the intent."

Lukas plays out that strategy with a tangible example. "With a product like our VIVA paper towels, we know that when women touch and feel VIVA towels, they immediately understand the differences and benefits between VIVA and other paper towels," she notes.

> If "feel" is the intent, then we need to market in ways that get the product literally into the hands of our female consumers. Television advertising is not tactile, so why assume television will be effective, even though it's been part of our marketing for years. An actual hands-on experience with VIVA seems like a more meaningful channel for marketing that product.

I applaud Kimberly-Clark for not just exploring, but also acting on the notion that there may be better ways to reach female consumers. Many of the companies I spoke with still see a departure from the standard television ad as risky. To me, that is analogous to a young person saving for retirement in completely low-risk investments. The perception of risk is wrong. The real risk for the young investor is that inflation will outpace the "safe" returns. With marketers, the real risk is that those television ads, deemed to be safe marketing because they have been a mainstay, are

Questions Every Marketer or Business Owner Should Ask

- What aspect of my brand or business is most credible in the minds of my female consumers?

- Who am I engaging as spokespeople or ambassadors for my brand or business?

- Are my key messages relevant and short enough for busy women to grasp easily? Do they care? How do I know?

- What gaps might I have in my E-surround Programming? How can I fill them?

- Does my marketing have elements that are long-term relationship focused? Am I eliciting consumer feedback and then adapting based on that input?

- Am I offering solutions and positioning my brand or business as part of that solution?

- Is my brand or business helping to make the world a better place in some way that makes sense for my brand and for my consumers?

- Do I understand the power of women's voices in the online space and how those voices are affecting my brand? What am I doing about it?

being watched increasingly less frequently by female consumers. You are losing ground to competitors right now because women have turned off television ads in favor of more relevant communication.

IN-STORE AND BETWEEN FRIENDS

In addition to more "choiceful" channels to reach women, Lukas offers thoughts on what the near-term future will bring when it comes to better ways to reach female consumers.

"Packaging is more important than ever. Just like our communications, packaging should work for the consumer, not just the brand," she explains. "In those precious moments when a consumer is in-store making that real purchase decision, the package should help in a real way, not just be an efficient design full of 'bursts' that may not be helpful."

Consistent with the VIVA example, Lukas thinks more peer-to-peer or word-of-mouth efforts will become a wave of the future. "We know women are influenced more by sources they deem credible, their peers or like-minded women, and they are influenced less by pure advertising and experts that don't have a connection to them or the brand."

Lukas believes that in-store experiences can have a major impact, and that we'll see more of that type of marketing activity in the future. She anticipates more partnerships with retail customers to help consumers at the point of sale.

WOMEN WILL MAKE THE WORLD A BETTER PLACE WITH OR WITHOUT YOU

Like many of the other experts interviewed for this book, Lukas also sees far more environmental consciousness in the minds of female consumers.

"Sustainability, social responsibility, and making this world a better place are all on the minds of consumers today and will be for some time," she foresees.

> Women have been the conscience of this country for ages. They lead peacemaking as they see their sons being sent off to war. They are hugely sensitive to social issues as they impact their families. Today, women are not relying on governments or big organizations to make changes when it comes to making this world a better place. They see it as a personal responsibility.

Between the current power of the purse, the growing connectedness of online communities and women's nature to care for others, I believe Lukas' prediction is tremendously insightful.

Given her powerful command of the marketing-to-women arena, I was interested to find out what one "must-do" she would recommend to marketers so they can better reach multi-minding female consumers.

"Women now have an unprecedented ability to have a voice online. Marketers must understand the digital space and what the power of those voices means," she says. "Brands must be prepared, responsive, transparent, and agile when it comes to the online world and the world in general today. Brands cannot stand apart. They must understand how they can be a good and meaningful brand."

Brands and businesses that engage Lukas' philosophy will certainly be on their way to finding better approaches to reach female consumers.

M^2 Must-Dos

- ✓ Engage the four phases of marketing to women—Credibility, Quick-Connect Messaging, E-surround Programming, and Consistent Confirmation.
- ✓ Engage relevant and credible spokespeople to serve as messengers to women for your brand or business.

✓ Distill your messages to the briefest, most relevant level and then provide a source for exploring more details, such as a Web site or brochure.

✓ Explore the channels for reaching women that are truly connecting with them today, without assumptions.

✓ Plan a holistic and "choiceful" portfolio of touch points for your marketing so your brand or business is where your female consumer is.

✓ Include elements in your marketing that will enable it to build an ongoing relationship with your consumers.

Chapter Ten

What Really Matters? Credibility

Credibility. It is the most important filter used by multi-minding women. With a schedule that allows little time for any one activity, multi-minding women use credibility as a necessary shortcut to making purchasing decisions. Credibility means less research is needed. Since most women conduct varying levels of research before making a purchase, credibility helps them save time. Without credibility, your message is just one of many that gets tossed by the wayside.

Multi-minding women have a lot on their mind. In fact, Ketchum research showed that 58 percent of women ages 25 to 54 have much more on their minds than they did just five years ago. Surprisingly, that percentage is a substantial 18 percent higher than that of the total public, 20 percent higher than men ages 25 to 54, and 35 percent higher than men in general, according to the Ketchum study.[1]

In addition, the study found that women 25 to 54 are more likely to have a variety of thoughts competing for their attention as they juggle multiple tasks. It is easy to understand why these thoughts also are more easily distracted. This distraction leads to less time and decreased desire to consume media—a primary conduit for commercial communications. Take a look at these statistics from the same study:[2]

- Fifty-nine percent of women surveyed "rarely" or "never" read a newspaper from beginning to end.
- Slightly more than half (51 percent) "frequently" watch a television program from start to finish, compared with 60 percent of men, and 55 percent of the total public.
- Just 47 percent "frequently" listen to the radio for more than 30 minutes straight versus 62 percent of their male counterparts.

With so much mental activity and so little time to digest messages, credibility is the key to overcoming these obstacles of today's multi-minding mind-set.

WHO HAS THE MOST CREDIBILITY?

The survey found that women trust experts, friends, family members, and editorial media as the most credible sources of information. These sources provide a green light for women who are making purchasing decisions. Without the okay from a trusted source, more time is needed to investigate the options. Time is not something you or a multi-minding consumer have on your side.

Furthermore, Hartman Group research shows that "sources of information can be contradictory and overwhelming, but consumers are more compelled to believe they have to learn what to do from others, and not expect it all to be natural and intuitive."[3]

As a result, women are seeking information that will assist them, but with so little time, they need help identifying what to read, listen to, or watch. A primary factor that facilitates that identification is credibility, which is a key to enabling focus for a multi-minding woman. It is a trusted "express lane" to what she needs, including time-saving measures. Credibility serves as a filter, or a test, through which she will sift all of the information vying for her attention. The commercial information becomes much less commercial and much more relevant, if it comes to her by way of friends and family, experts, and the editorial media, both online and offline.

ENGAGING THE CREDIBILITY OF FRIENDS AND FAMILY

If friends and family are cited as *the* most credible source of information, then how do you go about tapping into those sources on your behalf? Many marketers are currently discussing this topic. How do you do it? Is it worth it? How can I justify it? These questions are percolating in the minds of marketers and the media.

Given that friends and family, or word-of-mouth marketing, is such a hot topic, it is worth consulting an expert. To gain some perspective on this topic, I talked to Paul Rand, president and chief executive officer of the Zócalo Group in Chicago, and an executive committee and board member for the Word of Mouth Marketing Association (WOMMA).

"Because of the credibility associated with friends and family, word-of-mouth marketing is becoming an industry unto itself. Not only is a new industry being born, but recent research shows that word-of-mouth will be one of the fastest-growing communications disciplines for the foreseeable future," Rand notes. "Brands are realizing that many of the marketing tools they used to count on are not delivering the way they need them to today."

Headlines in leading marketing and business trade publications validate the points made by Rand. Companies like Kellogg's and Kimberly-Clark are reducing the size of their traditional media buys on television and replacing that traditional marketing with more activities that engage consumers.

"Companies have got to make an impact in consumer engagement and fast," says Rand. "If you do not have a high level of engagement, you lose."

With all of the talk about word-of-mouth marketing, buzz marketing, guerilla marketing, and the many other terms used to describe and market the idea of tapping into friends and family, Rand offers some sound advice.

"What's important for marketers to realize is that word of mouth must be sustainable to be credible," he says. "It's not just an ad or an in-market event. It comes down to driving sustainable conversations that lead to long-term relationships and business. Buzz is not credibility. It must be a holistic approach, especially with women."

Rand's comments about the need for sustainability and a holistic approach are consistent with the core tenets of successfully marketing to women in general. It is not a one-shot deal that you then check off your list. It is an ongoing effort aimed at building and evolving real relationships. Real relationships do not happen overnight, but rather they require ongoing attention, frequent connections, good listening skills, and an ability to adapt and change.

IF YOU DON'T DO IT, SOMEONE ELSE WILL

Rand predicts a growing divide will emerge between the companies that get it and those that do not when it comes to building credibility through sustainable word-of-mouth activities:

> I see a land grab ahead with those who are first to market at successfully and truly engaging consumers being the winners. Those who wait will have double the work. If your competition has formed a relationship with someone who is a high-value consumer for your product, you first need to break up the relationship and then establish yourself as a worthy replacement. That's a harder job than engaging the consumer at the outset.

Credibility, indeed, is the foundation of any communications program that needs to succeed with multi-minding women. As I thought about all of the situations in which credibility is the most important and most difficult to achieve, one area came to the forefront.

THE ULTIMATE TEST OF CREDIBILITY

Imagine building credibility in this marketing environment: Time is limited. Stakes are high. The competition is intense and can be ruthless. Budgets are sizable, but must support a 24/7 effort. Smear campaigns are abundant. Sound like what you face? Add to that scenario daily opinion polls on how well you are doing your job. Media, bloggers, and the general public scrutinize your every move.

Sounds like a movie, but it is real life in the political arena. Perhaps the most grueling and public test of credibility in marketing is an election. The candidate is the product and the success or failure of the marketing efforts is determined in a single day.

In many ways, political marketing is actually ahead of mainstream marketing. The marketing, the communications, and especially the messages are based on extensive research. Great care is taken to understand the target audiences and to talk directly with them. Pilot programs and test markets are used to test and refine ideas before they reach the national stage. An integrated mix of advertising, editorial media, direct mail, word-of-mouth marketing, blogger relations, Internet work, media tours, town hall meetings, and more are combined to create a comprehensive marketing program. All of the tactics have a specific and measureable return on investment in the form of votes.

While there is a common focus and ongoing debate on the negative aspects of political marketing, the strategic process and implementation are extremely sophisticated. Because time is limited to get to the desired result, decisions and changes are made quickly, always with a tangible goal in mind. Imagine if marketers approached communications campaigns more like they do in politics.

As marketers, we can learn a great deal from successful political campaigns, especially when it comes to dealing with multi-minding women. Representing the current base, or about 60 percent, of the Democratic Party and a desirable target for the Republicans, women are playing a larger and more important role in elections than ever before. That is why both political parties are actively courting them.

Despite all of these efforts and many more along the road of the presidential campaign trail, political candidates on both sides of the aisle have trouble courting women. The key to that difficulty is credibility—a "must have" with multi-minding women.

At the end of the day, though, the choices are limited in an election. New and improved products are not introduced to the marketplace on a regular basis from which to choose. If a woman is going to vote, she compares the candidates on the facts, the issues, the messages, the personalities, and, often in her subconscious, the relative credibility of her choices. She then casts a vote.

It is a fascinating process ending at a certain moment in time with a "buy" or "buy someone else" decision.

IMPORTANT LESSONS WE CAN LEARN FROM POLITICAL MARKETING

Susan Molinari, the former president and chief executive officer of the Washington Group and the former highest-ranking woman in Congress, has seen it all in political campaigns. She has been the winning candidate and has strategized at the highest levels of politics for some of the most high-profile campaigns in recent history.

She can be described as a smart legislator, an amazingly networked business woman, a real player on the national political landscape, a sought-after television commentator, a doting mother, and a great woman. It is a privilege for me to share her astute take on what is being done in politics to reach multi-minding women and how those tools can be repurposed by consumer marketers.

"There is no time for fairy dust. There is only so much time to prime the market and all 'buying' decisions are made on one day," says Molinari. "There is no room for something that cannot drive the desired return on investment."

A shift in the 2004 presidential election occurred as a clear focus on female voters emerged.

"Women are taking on increasing importance in elections for both Republican and Democratic candidates," notes Molinari. "President Bush's election in 2004 really seemed to make a shift in a focus on female votes. 'Security moms' had an impact on the election, and campaigns since then have had a much bigger focus on female voters."

That focus on female voters appears to be alive and well. In preparation for the 2008 presidential election, Hillary Clinton hired six full-time staffers devoted to women's outreach.[4] Barack Obama created a women's policy committee and had a key, maybe *the* key influencer with the female audience, Oprah Winfrey, on his side. And Sarah Palin embodied the idea of multi-minding women.

"Women voters seem to make their decisions based on the issues, as well as the personalities and personal issues of the candidates," Molinari adds. "If what the candidate is saying does not match with the personal perception of the candidate, it creates cognitive dissonance or a lack of credibility in the mind of a female voter, so the personal credibility of the candidate is paramount with women."

Women's intuition or ability to smell a rat comes to the surface in political campaigns. Women, more than men, seem to sense the small, but important, inconsistencies that deteriorate the credibility that is so important to female consumers, whether they are buying a grocery product or electing a president.

ONE SIZE DOES *NOT* FIT ALL

"There is no one-size-fits-all message or campaign that will work with women," stresses Molinari. "While education, homeland security, and the environment typically resonate with women, it's different for each candidate. It should come from who they authentically are."

The same can be said for brands or companies. One-size marketing does not fit all and campaigns that do not truly reflect that brand or company will be perceived as "not quite right" in the minds of female consumers.

Take, for instance, an automobile company that communicates all of the advantages and safety upgrades of a new car, making it a perfect choice for a family. Those messages intrigue a mom, who perceives them to be relevant to her needs and sees them verified in an article in one of her favorite magazines. When she and her husband walk into the dealership, however, the gleaming glass and chrome furniture, the all-male sales force, and a lack of anything or anyone that is child-friendly negates all of the positive messages that initially drove her awareness and interest. Despite all of the marketing effort and expense, there is no sale.

Not only is there no sale made, but also the woman is angry. If you had never led her to believe that the car was perfect for a family and she just happened to like it, no problem. Yet, you led her to believe one thing and then did not deliver. You wasted her time and disappointed her. She has about 10 close friends, talks to about 20 other parents in her local parent-teacher organization, works with 40 colleagues, and is an active member of Clubmom.com and Cafemom.com. How many other women does she have the potential to share her disappointment with? At least 5,000.

If that same car company had engaged its target audience in more aspects of its business, it would have known, long before it disappointed consumers, that its showroom experience did not match its communications. There are ways, which are now being used in the political arena, to do just that.

MICRO-TARGETING DELIVERS MACRO RESULTS

"One of the places that private industry could really learn from politics is in audience targeting," notes Molinari. "In fact, some political campaigns are using a sophisticated, effective and advanced method of targeting called micro-targeting."

While mainstream marketers are still targeting mass audiences, especially with women, micro-targeting focuses on small groups of influential and active voters. The targeted groups could be as small as a single neighborhood. The micro-targeted approach is the antithesis of the national campaigns still being conducted by brands and businesses on a regular basis.

It is a different way of thinking that is worth exploring for mainstream marketers and one that could prove incredibly effective with multi-minding women.

"It's not a science, but micro-targeting is very thoughtful and thorough," Molinari adds.

> Voter participation is the foundation of this approach. Then, local focus groups and polling are conducted. Local media is studied, including what the leading newspapers, television, and radio stations are saying from an editorial standpoint. That research helps in the development of messages and identification of messengers. Then, the topics and issues are packaged for a national audience.

The micro-targeting approach described by Molinari is brilliant in its simplicity and ability to create a credible foundation for communications. It addresses some of the core tenets of reaching multi-minding women, which a great number of mainstream marketing campaigns ignore. And, it starts from the ground up. At the grassroots level, the messages are formed, tested, and tweaked. Leading trends and trendsetters are identified. Next, the messages that were built by the consumer, not the marketer (in this case, a candidate), are grown into a national platform.

I can tell you that is almost the exact opposite of what many marketers are doing today. By now, we have all heard of consumer-generated content. The micro-targeting approach enables consumer-generated content to be at the heart of the campaign, not just a superficial add-on, which, by the way, can be detected by a female consumer in an instant.

Identify specifically who your target audience is and where she lives, rather than trying to reach everyone. Get input and collect opinions directly from the women in your target—not just from national, quantitative studies that aggregate collective opinion. Understand the media that reach them on a local level, not just national television and newspapers with high reach and impressive circulation figures.

In the election process, this concentrated effort to know, understand, and communicate to a specific consumer results in a vote or "purchase" of the candidate. One of the biggest challenges facing marketers is determining what marketing communications activities actually drive the purchase. Imagine how much more effective marketers and business owners could be in driving purchasing decisions by engaging this approach.

Questions Every Marketer or Business Owner Should Ask

- How am I generating credibility for my product or service? Am I using friends and family, experts, and editorial media as credible messengers?

- What upcoming project do I have when I could test micro-targeting? What metrics will I use for pre- and postprogram measurement and evaluation?

- How can I operate on a more local level, even for national initiatives, at first, and then build to a national platform?

Because this type of marketing activity truly starts with the consumer, not the marketer, it has a much higher level of credibility, it is less commercial, and it really resonates with the consumer. Women today are inundated with information, but this approach creates credibility and makes the message a part of their life, not just another commercial, according to Molinari.

REAL AND VIRTUAL COMMUNITIES WIELD INFLUENCE

It used to be that women sought recommendations and advice from family and friends they spoke to in person—that call to your mom asking what medicine to use for a child's fever, that conversation over dinner with your sister about which lipstick lasted the longest, that over-the-fence exchange about a great recipe, and that cocktail hour with good girlfriends that covered everything from the best boutiques to the best attorney.

The key is that this exchange used to be based on those who physically lived near you or those you knew well enough to call on the phone. Women and moms today are physically farther away from their parents, relatives, and other support networks. Their busy schedules give them little time to rebuild those networks in their neighborhood and school communities.

With the bombardment of consumer information, a more transient society, and significant time constraints, more women are turning to less conventional sources, such as blogs, social networking sites, and Web sites, to get trusted information and recommendations. In fact, these interactive sites are becoming extended networks of friends and family. These virtual neighborhoods give women access to many other women who are in the same life stage as they are, making the topics and discussions *very* relevant to what they want to know and where they are in life.

Recent Hartman Group research finds that information gathered during Googling sessions, on community-centered listservs, and on national parenting sites plays a fundamental role in many households and in the decision-making processes about products, children's nutrition, medical advice, special-needs concerns, schools, and everyday parenting topics.[5]

If you are unsure about what to do with a sick child in the middle of the night, a host of mommy blogs and the online version of *Merck Manual* will provide advice. If you are unsure about whether you are considered rich or poor in New York City, Urbanbaby.com has a number of discussion threads to guide your self-assessment. If you are a working mom trying to manage your work and home life better, Mommytrackd.com, Hybridmom.com, Cafemom.com, and many, many others engage tens of thousands of women facing the same issues. If you cannot decipher a candidate's position on the issues that are important to you, try Glassbooth.com, which provides questions and filters to facilitate understanding.

These online tools and sites have been used by women for a number of years now and their popularity seems to be growing. It will be extremely interesting to evaluate the role of these sites, and in particular the blogs, in electing the president in 2008. In the 2004 election, blogs were on the cusp of mainstream adoption and participation. In 2008, just four years later, blogs have taken on quite a life of their own, rivaling mainstream political media in terms of influence and readership.

ELECTIONS AND THE BLOGOSPHERE

I asked Molinari about the impact bloggers will have in electing presidents in future elections. She says the 2008 presidential election was the first time that campaigns had to deal just as seriously and consistently with bloggers as they did with prominent news personalities who ask difficult questions.

"If women are turning to the blogosphere in droves for other types of information like healthcare, child-rearing and legal advice, it's likely to expect they will go there for political guidance," she explains.

The impact of bloggers is a relatively new dynamic in politics where established journalists and family and friends were primary sources of education, debate, and opinion-formation.

"The influence of close friends and family members may actually be diluted as women look more and more to online sources that they can access any time of the day or night when they have a few, uninterrupted minutes to explore the issues," Molinari speculates.

That is an interesting prediction and one that may hold true beyond the boundaries of political campaigns as women begin to think of their virtual communities as real friends and family. While a multi-minding woman increasingly may not get as much time as she would like to talk in person with her closest advisors—family and friends—it is more likely that she could grab a few uninterrupted minutes to explore a topic and recommendation in an online forum. That uninterrupted time online could, indeed, accelerate the impact of online influencers to the point that online becomes more influential than real, offline influencers.

M^2 Must-Dos

- ✓ Do "micro-targeting" on a local level. Pick a neighborhood that indexes high for your product. Conduct deep-drill polling and in-depth focus groups.
- ✓ Conduct local events and deliver local media.
- ✓ Use the local findings and trends to drive a national campaign, not the opposite.

Chapter Eleven

Time Is of the Essence: "Quick-Connect" Messages

Today, marketers do not have much margin for error when it comes to how much time they initially have to get a woman's attention. There is no time to lose, because her attention is gone before you know it. Multi-minding women do not have time, and they certainly are not going to wait. Many, many things are competing for the attention and mind share of female consumers and commercial messages are not at the top of that long list.

"Why is it that men can read an entire newspaper or magazine and all I can manage is a quick skim," Sandy wonders. "Actually, I prefer it that way. If you can't say it to me in a short paragraph, or better yet a few bullet points, don't bother."

Quickly connect or do not bother. Those are strong words and sound advice for marketers. Keep in mind that women 25 to 54 are more likely to report that they do not often have undivided time to consume media. Women are less likely than men to say that, on an average day, they frequently watch a television program from start to finish or listen to the radio for more than 30 minutes. Furthermore, these women are less likely than all groups—Americans, women, men, and men 25 to 54—to report that they frequently get to read a paper or magazine from start to finish, watch a television show from beginning to end, or listen to the radio for more than 30 minutes. In fact, more than half say they rarely or never read a paper from beginning to end or read a magazine from cover to cover.[1]

That declining attention to media is accompanied by much more multi-minding behavior in general. Almost 6 in 10 women say they have much more on their minds now, compared with five years ago. Remember, that is 18 percent higher than the total public, 20 percent higher than men 25 to 54, and 35 percent higher than men in general.[2]

IT'S NOT ABOUT A SECRET MESSAGE; IT'S THE
SECRET TO MESSAGING

The secret to messages that quickly connect is threefold. First, the message itself must be brief. The message must connect to something that is relevant to the consumer's life and, finally, it must be delivered by someone the consumer deems credible. These three concepts work together to quickly connect with a female consumer. This type of message merits her attention, if only for a few seconds, and paves the way for future messages, which are also part and parcel of the holistic approach.

Let's talk about brevity of message first. This concept is a tough one for many marketers. Understandably so, brands and businesses take great pride in their product or service, and want to share all of the great things their product or service can do. Claims, features, and benefits, new and improved, nutritional content, and many other details are communicated in the marketing. There is a time and place for details, as I will cover later in the chapter, but you cannot move a female consumer to in-depth exploration until you have initially caught her attention. As we know, her initial attention span is finite, as in seconds. Liken it to an invitation or introduction. You cannot say everything in an introduction, but you can pique interest that will open the door for the next communication.

Paid media, such as advertising, often enables a veritable barrage of messages to be included in 30-second spots or on a full-page ad. Having worked in the public relations business for two decades, I know these professionals have been guilty of long-form messaging, too. At Ketchum, we developed a proprietary set of messaging tools as part of the Ketchum Planning Process. These tools have enabled us to become much more adept at distilling messages to their essence, making the bite-size messages repeatable.

MESSAGES WITH A REAL-LIFE CONNECTION

In addition to brevity, a relevant connection to consumers' lives must be present. Who cares if something is new and improved, if the consumer did not care about it in the first place? Who cares about bits and bytes, if what the consumers want to know is whether they will be able to print their digital pictures? Who cares if you offer new hot breakfast food, if the nutritional content is poor? The message must connect to a consumer need, and she must clearly be able to identify that connection.

Let's go back to a key concept that Stacy DeBroff, founder of Mom Central, brought up earlier in the book. "You need to build messages around a core need or anxiety that will be relevant. If your brand can honestly help to solve one of those challenges, even in a small way, that's a golden message." It is that combination of message elevation and message relevance I addressed in previous chapters—message relevation. If your brand or business could craft its messages in such a way that elevates the message to a core need, it makes the brand relevant to the consumers' lives.

THE MESSENGER COULD KILL THE MESSAGE

With a brief, relevant message in hand, we now need to consider one more important factor, credibility of the messenger. Generally speaking, women consider friends and family, experts, and editorial media of all types, including print, television, and radio, to be the most credible sources of information. Therefore, an initial connection that happens via these sources is more likely to grab her immediate attention than a pure marketing message.

Given the most credible sources, brands and businesses of all types should be considering online and offline relationship building, word-of-mouth campaigns, influencer outreach, and editorial media relations as essential parts of their marketing efforts. Ask your target consumers who they consider to be their most credible sources when making a purchasing decision about your product or service. The input will help you prioritize your efforts using the most credible sources.

BRIEF, BUT . . .

There is a caveat to one part of this Quick-Connect Messaging theory. As you have probably picked up in different parts of this book, women like to do prepurchase research. That means providing details is important and has its rightful place in marketing to multi-minding women. Today, Web sites are often the most effective and efficient ways to provide details, answer questions, and customize information. Depending on your audience's age, location, comfort level with technology, and access to technology, other means of providing details via brochures, customer service 800 numbers, and product representatives also may be good choices.

Consider, too, the type of product you market. Bigger, more complex purchases often drive the desire for more research. For instance, research shows that women are more likely to research consumer electronics purchases (82 percent) than they are to research consumer-packaged goods (55 percent) or food purchases (47 percent). Women do report doing some or even a lot of research for food and consumer-packaged goods, however. This indicates that research is not out of the question for these categories, especially when it comes to health and wellness products.

In fact, three-quarters of women polled say they do research before making health and wellness decisions, and 7 out of 10 women usually read news about research and studies related to health and wellness. Another 7 out of 10 women say they always make time to learn more about health and nutrition for themselves or their families.[3] Keep in mind that mothers tend to research both consumer-packaged goods and food purchases more than nonmothers.

When making purchase decisions, women want to make informed decisions on large purchases, although smaller ones can be made on impulse. Mothers, more than women without children, say they rarely make impulsive purchases (37 percent versus 31 percent, respectively), but nonmothers are more likely than mothers to do research before making big purchases (76 percent versus 70 percent, respectively).[4] Given that mothers tend to think of others' needs before their own and multi-mind to an even higher degree than nonmothers in the same age categories, these findings make perfect sense and serve as good guidelines when providing details to women both with and without children.

The time that marketers have to connect with consumers is being examined from a number of perspectives. *Stopwatch Marketing*, a book by John Rosen and AnnaMaria Turano that focuses on consumers' internal stopwatches and the window of opportunity for selling, connects the idea of risk of the purchase to how much time a consumer will devote to engaging in the purchase.[5] I can tell you that a multi-minding woman's internal stopwatch will not stop for a second unless the messages quickly connect through brevity, relevance, and credible messengers.

I thought it would be helpful to provide a couple of Quick-Connect Messaging examples in a variety of categories.

GREEN AND BROWNE

First, an interview with Gay Browne, founder of Greenopia, will shed light on the hot topic of green products, and how Quick-Connect Messaging applies to this fast-growing category. Growth and "green washing" are frequent topics of media coverage and conversation, so I thought green marketing would be a dynamic category and interesting filter to examine Quick-Connect messages.

Browne, a lifelong asthmatic, began to search for ways to improve her environment and take better care of herself and her children. She started from the inside out by choosing all-natural alternatives for everything from nutritional habits to bed sheets. In her experience researching and working with green home developers, interior designers, and furniture dealers, she realized there were a wealth of green options, but not one simple resource to find them. In response, she developed Greenopia to provide a resource to help people like herself make choices to green up their lives on a daily basis.

Greenopia: *The Urban Dweller's Guide to Green Living* is available in print and on the Web at Greenopia.com. With exhaustively researched, nonpaid listings, the *Greenopia* guide provides consumers with a resource to locate a wide range of local green businesses, services, and organizations in metropolitan cities. Browne has created a unique, easy-to-understand Green Leaf award system that rates the level of organic and sustainable products that a listed company provides to the consumer.

She shared some astute perspectives for the marketing of green products to women now and in the near future. Given the onslaught of green products of every type and the resulting confusion in the marketplace, Browne's comments can apply to almost every product or business.

"Over the years, I have seen that women and college-aged kids are the driving force in the green movement," Browne observes.

> What companies need to know is that women are not buying products because they are green. Almost unanimously, in talking with women who buy green, they are doing it out of concern for personal health, a healthier home, or the health of a child. Health, home, and children are the topics that women jump on, and messages related to those areas will enable a green product to quickly connect with a woman.

According to a MomConnection study released by *Parenting* magazine, Browne is right on. Moms are clearly motivated, receptive, and are the primary decision makers in the choice to go green. The research shows that 71 percent of moms are more likely than nonmoms to go green *if* they have information about how it will benefit their family. Furthermore, 79 percent say that moms are the gatekeepers of green for the family, deciding which products will be purchased for the household.[6]

The study also notes that only about half of moms are even aware that green brand choices are available in common categories like surface cleaners, laundry detergent, diapers, paper goods, and storage bags. Clearly, the necessary marketing is missing here. Moms need to know more about their options and good reasons to go green, which the study cites as kids, her home, and the environment. Media coverage often drives interest in certain topics.

"Women are alarmed when news comes out about questionable food sources, toxic ingredients in toys, or tainted food. Often times, motivation to go green comes from fear that their health or the health of their family could be compromised," Browne notes.

An emerging segment of "eco-moms" is concerned about almost everything from the potential toxicity issues with children's toys to water conservation. According to a story in the *New York Times*, eco-mom gatherings are becoming almost as common as the Tupperware parties of the 1970s. These women not only discuss the latest news, but also share information on what their families are doing to protect their health and the environment. True to form with most multi-minding women today, eco-moms share information in person, as well as online, and a growing number of Web sites provide mom-friendly information and resources. Much like Browne, the eco-moms' interest in green seems to stem from a desire to personally lead a healthier life.

Based on my research at Ketchum, health is a big part of how women are defining their success today in general. In fact, 8 in 10 women feel that being healthy and having healthy children (82 and 81 percent, respectively) are the top qualities that define success. When you combine those research findings with Browne's perspectives, it seems that buying green contributes to a woman's overall feeling of success as a woman and as a mother. Protecting her family and the environment makes women and moms, in particular, feel good and successful in life.

The key to igniting the connection between multi-minding women and green is one-on-one relevance.

"There must be a personal connection. Green must have a relationship with the female consumer," notes Browne. "Connecting green products to family, health, and home makes it personal and relevant."

There is no doubt that green is white hot. With each passing day, you see more products and marketing of products that focus on being green in some way or some dimension of green, such as sustainability. "Manufacturers are racing to get products out there in the marketplace because green is such a hot topic," Browne says.

That influx of information certainly ramps up the competition, as well as confusion, in the minds of consumers given that there is not yet one generally accepted way to measure "green." Green-washing is the term being used to describe what some companies do to imply an exaggerated sense of "greenness." Browne uses "integrity" as her measure of what women want and what companies should do when it comes to green.

"Women are smart and want to know the truth. It's insulting to be lied to. Don't say your product is environmental if it's not," advises Browne. "Be intelligent, be honest, and be transparent" when it comes to green claims.

Browne tells a story that illustrates her point:

Think about this common scenario. Your child has a play date scheduled and then comes down with a cold. You could show up at the play date without telling the other child's mother. It's not a serious illness, so the play date would likely go on, but the other child's mother would be irritated. It would negatively impact the relationship.

She's now skeptical and would think twice about another play date. But if you call ahead and alert the mother, most times she would just say. "Fine. It's just a cold." She'd very much appreciate your honesty. It's the same concept in marketing green. The expectation is not that you'll be perfect, but you must be honest and upfront.

As a mom myself, I think this story perfectly describes the needed level and style of honesty.

Some marketers stretch their green claims to make them seem better in the eyes of the consumer. That stretch will do more damage in the long term than any benefits the false claims will provide in the short-term, though. Multi-minding women with little time for commercial messages and a keen ability to smell a rat will not give you multiple chances for their attention.

So how can you get their attention even if you are not perfectly green? Browne advocates the one-step-at-a-time approach. "Marketers must be realistic. One step at a time is OK. I applaud that approach as long as there is a commitment to continue to evolve. Just be sure to market what you can legitimately claim."

I asked Browne to speculate a bit about the future of green marketing and what she sees coming down the pike in terms of marketing green to women.

"Women don't just wake up one morning and decide to buy green. They are making choices about green one product at a time." She returns to her original premise as a valid concept for the future. "Health, home, and children are of highest concern to women and often some of the first areas in which women start to buy green."

Browne sees several areas as ripe for more choices that include green. "Beauty products, hair care, and clothes are all categories where I expect to see more green alternatives. Eco labels for textiles are starting to pop up now with organic cotton, hemp, and bamboo being used."

True to the one-step-at-a-time approach, Browne sees traditional and known manufacturers adding healthier alternatives, while they still market more traditional and perhaps less green versions of their products.

"It's a natural cycle. You can't just replace every product with a greener version overnight," she says. "Consumers recognize that reality."

Browne also sees the future power of women and moms banding together to support causes, products, and businesses that relate to health, home, and children.

"If moms decided tomorrow to protest the lack of nutrition in white bread, it would be gone or replaced with a better alternative. Women will continue to find more ways to exchange opinions and experiences and a lot of that will be done on the Internet." In fact, in the future, Browne and Greenopia.com will begin to harness consumer feedback on green topics and products, and then make that information available to all via Web site ratings.

Browne provides sage advice when marketing green products to multi-minding women:

> Make the product convenient to find. Women are in the habit of buying things they know. They will reach for the same apples in the same place in the produce section unless they readily see the organic apples right beside them. I think we'll soon see less separation between organic/green products and other products in the supermarket. You are making women think twice, something they don't have time to do, if you have the same types of products in different sections. Whole Foods has done a masterful job of making organic convenient.

That convenience speaks to a marketing "must-do" that Browne advocates—do the homework for the consumer.

"In this age of nano-second attention spans, you must get your messages across quickly. Help women reduce the time it takes to research a certain topic," she recommends.

> Educate them in a quick and easy way. For example, Whole Foods has greatly reduced the amount of label reading that shoppers need to do by offering only products that meet their standards. Women love that they can have a more pleasant shopping experience because Whole Foods has done the work for them and they are willing to pay more for that valuable time savings.

From "green" to red and white—wine, that is. A product long known for its complexity, wine is another category that is actively marketed to the ever-desirable multi-minding woman. If you are a wine aficionado, you embrace the thought of pouring through wine reviews to find tastes and deals. You love to read about French and American oak barrels, hints of melon and berries, and the best years for particular vintages.

But remember earlier in this chapter when we talked about brevity, relevance, and credibility? If you are among the typical multi-minding women who represent a huge volume of potential wine sales, what you likely want is a wine that complements a meal you are making for others, tastes good, and does not require much time to decipher. These women probably will pick up a recommendation from a visit to a friend's house, not from a wine review.

Leslie Sbrocco, author of *Wine for Women* (2003), understands the reality of multi-minding women buying wine and the importance of Quick-Connect Messaging. In her book, she recognizes that wine is important to women mainly in the context of serving it to friends and family and in connection with a meal. With that insight, Sbrocco's book greatly simplifies wine selection by connecting wines to something most

---

Questions Every Marketer or Business Owner Should Ask

- Are the key messages about my product or business brief?

- Are my key messages connected to a relevant topic or issue on the life of my female consumer?

- Which messengers are the most credible to my female audience for my particular product or business, and are my messages being delivered by those credible messengers?

- Do I provide resources (Web site, brochure) where my female consumer can thoroughly research my product or business? Do I connect her to other, unbiased resources to aid in her research?

- Am I doing as much of the homework as possible for my consumer, enabling her to educate herself and save time?

---

women are oh-so-familiar with—clothing. By relating a potentially complex decision to something women know well, she has created an ingenious system of Quick-Connect Messaging for wine and women.

Wine can be a mystery. Most women are not interested in unraveling the entire mystery, but rather figuring out how to share wine with family and friends. Sbrocco makes "building the essential wine wardrobe" easy by equating Chardonnay to a little black dress, Red Zinfandel to black leather pants, Pinot Gris to basic jeans, and my personal favorite, Sangiovese to Italian heels.[7] She translates her immense knowledge into accessible, practical, and friendly advice that makes wine fun, not intimidating.

FROM GREEN TO GREENS

Quick-Connect Messaging is not reserved for products like energy-saving light bulbs and wine. Travel and leisure activities and destinations, such as country clubs, are other services for which Quick-Connect Messaging can be engaged. As tax deductions for country club memberships have declined, so has the number of members, who traditionally have been male. With the lion's share of the family entertainment and leisure activity decisions always having been made by women, country clubs would be smart to court women and to position their facilities as places not just for men to golf with their clients or buddies. These clubs could have tremendous appeal to women as family activity centers where foursomes can be families and the woman of the house can simplify her day with a casual post-golf or -swim dinner at the club.

Several years ago, my family and I joined a club specifically because of the message that the club's tagline delivered: "Where Families Come to Play." What a great concept. The message was concise and relevant to me and my husband because we want recreational options that can involve the whole family. Children are welcome. Adults and children can learn and play golf together. A strong junior golf program enables kids to learn from professionals. Everyone who works there, whether in the pro shop, at the pool, in the kitchen, or on staff, is welcoming to adults and children alike. We love it.

That simple and effective message attracted our family and many others to the club, whose positioning is still a rarity, even though such clubs could stand to grow considerably by courting the person who wields the most influence over family leisure—moms. With this club in particular, the family-friendly messages and atmosphere carry throughout the facility except for one place, the women's golf locker room. Ironically, a sign that reads "no children under 16 permitted in women's locker room" is taped to the door of the locker room. What's a mother of children who are under 16 years old to do: leave the toddler at the bar or at the curb while she showers and changes?

After great work to create messages that quickly connect through brevity and relevance, the door sign erodes the credibility that they work so hard to maintain. What a shame. It is a testament to the holistic approach that is needed to effectively communicate with multi-minding women. You cannot park your message at the door.

M^2 Must-Dos

- ✓ Enable your messages to quickly connect through brevity, relevance, and credibility of messenger.
- ✓ Provide a way for women to dig deeper into the details of your product or business, especially if the product is complex or expensive.
- ✓ Help women draw comparisons between your product and something they may be more familiar with to streamline the time they need to understand it
- ✓ Do the homework for the consumer. Make it easy for her to research or become more educated.

Chapter Twelve

The 360-Degree "E-surround" Method to Reach Women

"It seemed like everywhere I was, I saw or heard something about Dove's campaign for real beauty," Tara recalls.

> My friend sent me a link to the Web site, I saw ads in my favorite magazines, the videos on YouTube were terrific, and I read an article about how the campaign is really committed to building self-esteem in girls. My sister and I have talked about real beauty and how refreshing it is to see realistic images of women. As a mother of two girls, I think the campaign is relevant and I see it everywhere.

Many woman reacted to the Dove campaign in that same way. The messages were credible and relevant, and were delivered to women via a variety of channels that were part and parcel of their daily lives. The campaign successfully engaged multi-minding female consumers because it became part of their daily life, not an add-on or a commercial interruption.

Multi-minding women, likely the target audience for your brand or business, are juggling the many dimensions of their busy lives. They rarely give undivided attention to any one item and clearly do not have the willingness or desire to give their precious time to commercial messages. In previous chapters, we have covered a number of the key cornerstones to better reach multi-minding women. Credibility and messages that quickly connect are absolutely essential in marketing to women today. They are not the only keys, however.

Many of the experts in this book have espoused the importance of a holistic approach. I will say it again: there is not a single magic-bullet solution to effectively market to women. The secret is in the holistic approach, which I will address in this chapter. While I have seen many brands make great strides, few have achieved a sufficient mix of meeting the consumer with credibility and quick-connect messaging.

IT'S HIT OR MISS, UNLESS IT'S HOLISTIC

Given the demands on a woman's time, she absolutely is going to miss your messages, especially if you communicate through a single medium, one that she does not consider credible, or in venues that do not intersect with her life. It is not necessary to completely surround the consumer as much as it is necessary to connect with her via multiple, relevant touch points.

Consider, for example, a car dealership that spends a great deal of money advertising via 30-second ads on daytime television and radio. The dealership is spending a significant amount of money and the content and images in the ads are on target. However, with more than 70 percent of women today working outside of the home, only a percentage of the target audience is watching or listening. The women included in that percentage are probably doing or thinking about something else, even if the television or radio is on. By investing all of the marketing dollars into the broadcast medium, even with a significant spend, the dealership likely has missed more of its target than it has reached. In addition, that ad campaign, without companion communications coming from word of mouth, experts, or online sources, is not nearly as credible. Without a more holistic approach, you will miss more women than you reach.

We know from the seminal research on multi-minding women that there are four especially credible sources of information for female consumers—equals (family and friends), editors (as in editorial media), experts (which will differ category by category), and entertainment (celebrities, sports marketing, popular culture). Ideally, a campaign should include all four of these "e" groups, although to differing degrees, depending on the product category. I call it "E-surround Programming."

E-SURROUND YOUR FEMALE CONSUMER

E-surround Programming, much like the overarching concept of marketing to women, is about a holistic approach. Single-channel approaches are bound to fail. Between multi-tasking and multi-minding, today's female consumer is busier than ever and you must meet her where she is, not where she used to be, to effectively reach her.

With more than 90 percent of the women polled saying they turn to family and friends as the most credible source of information, engaging online and offline peers has become critically important. Many brands and businesses, though, have not yet activated such activity in their marketing plans. According to research sponsored by TNS Media Intelligence/Cymfony, senior marketing executives in several countries agree that the use of social media for corporate, brand, and product marketing is not a passing fad.

In fact, nearly 50 percent believe it is a vital component of corporate communications that should be monitored at the executive level and allocated significant resources. In addition, 95 percent believe social media will grow in significance over the next five years. When asked about the uses of social media, respondents endorsed it as a strategic tool to gain consumer insights (37 percent), build brand awareness (21 percent), and increase customer loyalty (18 percent).[1] There is still a great deal of debate over word of mouth, how to implement it and how to measure it, but I would put it at the top of the learning agenda list no matter what your concerns.

Experts, or influencers, represent another area of sources that women view as being the most credible. These experts vary category by category. If you market a food brand, nutritionists or dietitians will be seen by women as credible. Better yet, if consumers hear or see a quote in support of your product from one of these experts, it is a powerful endorsement. If you are a hair salon, a well-known stylist or colorist at the salon who has worked with notable clients would be a viable expert. If you market a green cleaning product, a partnership with a reputable environmental group would provide expert support.

When using experts in marketing that focuses on moms, consider engaging a relevant, credentialed expert who is also a mom. According to the Intelligence Group's Mom Intelligence Report, a down-to-earth expert who is a mom is an ideal choice.[2] In selecting an expert who is a mom, you enable connections on two levels, doubling your relevance.

Editorial, nonpaid media are immensely credible with female consumers. The content of news stories online, in print, and in a broadcast format is consistently ranked more credible than the paid media. Ideally, the nonpaid and paid media would work together as pieces of the holistic approach, each reinforcing the other. The beauty of editorial media is the number of relevant and credible options.

Research tells us that local media outlets (print and broadcast) also are credible with women. That makes sense given those outlets contain information about the consumers' local community. Interestingly, many marketers of national products do not focus on local media, but rather emphasize coverage in national outlets to reach large numbers of women. Local market media relations add a credible layer of coverage that should not be ignored.

National media, like magazines, online sites, newspapers, and television shows, are also highly credible. Women are still reading, although in bite-size pieces and not in one sitting, more traditional women's magazines and are flocking to online sites like iVillage. These national media outlets reach millions of women every day and have adapted over time to maintain the readership of time-pressed women. With the holistic approach in mind, an ideal campaign would secure both national and key market local media. Typically, editorial media initiatives are achieved through public relations.

The credibility of individual entertainers or celebrities may be questionable, but women are undeniably influenced by entertainment, including athletes, movie stars, and television personalities. Popular culture is an influential source for women, especially in categories such as fashion, fitness, baby gear, certain foods and beverages, some durable goods, and entertaining.

Because the cost of celebrities often sets off alarm bells in the budget, it is not necessary to hire a high-paid spokesperson. Some companies, like POM Wonderful with its pomegranate juice, and a number of baby gear businesses, have seeded their products with celebrities as a way to get unpaid endorsements. Fashion houses routinely outfit movie stars on the red carpets of important events, like the Academy Awards. Products ranging from champagne to cameras are provided in the celebrity gift bags at such events. A resulting photo in an entertainment or fashion magazine of a celebrity showcasing your product is worth far more in influence than the resources needed to include that same celebrity in a paid advertisement.

Of course, the magic occurs when you can communicate through a combination of the most relevant sources, including equals, experts, editorial media, and entertainment. Few brands or businesses seem to successfully achieve the necessary combined approach. Dove's Campaign for Real Beauty, the example cited at the beginning of this chapter, epitomizes the holistic approach. The messengers, real women, were credible. The messages of "real beauty" and "self-esteem" connected immediately with women. Equals, experts, editorial media, and entertainment were all included in the campaign execution. Importantly, the campaign lived through updates, innovative online videos, a cause marketing tie-in, and the consistent involvement of real women.

SPECIAL K IS A SPECIAL CASE

Another great example is Kellogg's Special K, a brand that resonates with women using a holistic approach in both its range of products and its marketing. Credible messengers have included celebrity fitness instructors and female consumers. The cereal's simple, relevant message of being a weight-management partner and creating "a better me" hit home with women. The advertising portrays real women in real eating situations. Online partnerships provide real forums for discussion. The brand has succeeded in getting women to talk to each other, engaging fitness and fashion experts, achieving stellar editorial media coverage in a host of publications and shows, and becoming part of our popular culture with megabrand status.

Approaching the $1 billion mark in sales, Special K is synonymous with realistic weight management and is clearly succeeding with its female consumers. Mark Baynes, chief marketing officer at Kellogg's and a thought-leader in the marketing world, has shepherded Special K's evolution. When I talked with him, he had some interesting insights, predictions, and advice to share that are as relevant for marketers of a megabrand like Special K as they are for a smaller brand or business.

In talking with Baynes, I readily noticed his passion for Kellogg's products and the effective manner in which they are marketed.

"I think there are two primary reasons why Special K is so successful," he notes. "First, Special K strongly delivers some of the best-tasting food in the weight-management category. While most diets require denial and deprivation, Special K provides 'substitute without sacrifice' weight management. The food is exceptional." That concept is critical to Special K's success because, as anyone who has ever watched their weight knows, bad-tasting diet foods or taste fatigue can be the death of a diet.

"Second, most diet brands scream 'I want to lose weight.' Women don't want to be seen in public using a diet product or something that overtly suggests they need to lose weight," he adds.

> Special K has more of a handbag quality. It's something you are not embarrassed to carry around or have on your desk. It's realistic, helping women lose those five or six pounds that make them feel better. K is simply "a better me" for the consumer. It's not a magic bullet and does not promise to help someone lose 20 or 30 pounds. The brand wins with women because it is realistic.

The word "realistic" was used repeatedly by the experts I interviewed for this book. Realistic images of women. Realistic lives. Experts understand the realization that women are constantly trying to do their best and do not want to be compared with unrealistic images or portrayals. Special K has created immense equity with women, in part, because it fits into a real, daily diet—a diet without any strange or unknown foods that the consumer must eat. Importantly with multiminding women, Special K products are readily available in a place they visit regularly, supermarkets, so there are no hassles associated with clubs or going to special locations.

MARKETING EVOLUTION UNDERPINS K'S CURRENT SUCCESS

Baynes provides a relevant perspective on the history of how Special K has communicated with its female consumers.

"In the 1990s, we had clichéd images of women on the beach in swimsuits. Those images and the rest of the marketing were simply pushed out to the consumers. It was not a dialogue," he says. "We know much more today about how to make the brand relevant to women. Our marketing and communications are much more realistic and holistic."

A holistic approach is critical to effectively connecting with multi-minding women. Today's female consumers are busy multi-tasking and multi-minding, and they are bound to miss your product or service if you do not market holistically. Baynes refers to this phenomenon as "an attention-deficit economy." He advises, "You need to lead with relevant content and then enter the brand into that conversation."

The marketing for Special K has been masterful in marrying a holistic, consistent approach with relevant content that strengthened its image as an all-day weight-management partner for women. In 2007, for example, the brand kicked off the year with the launch of Special K20 Protein Water, as well as protein meal and snack bars, with fitness expert Harley Pasternak. Early 2007 also marked the launch of the highly rated Chocolatey Delight, providing a tasty, late-night snacking option.

As swimsuit season approached, the celebrity fitness expert reminded women how Special K protein products could help them get into shape for the summer season, a key trigger moment for women managing their weight. The brand then worked with a registered dietitian to help women "take back breakfast." By regularly eating a cereal like Special K, women are more likely to have a lower body mass index.

In the fall as women start to think about new apparel for the season, fashion expert Robert Verdi teamed with the brand to help women "fall" into new stylish jeans by dropping one size in two weeks. During the temptation-ridden holiday season, women learned holiday defense strategies for eating right and avoiding snacking pitfalls.

The brand helped women through key "moments of truth" throughout each day and during the year when diets and weight-management plans typically derail.

"We know now that simple, intuitive tips that are instructive and practical resonate much more with our consumers than those stereotypical swimsuit images. Special K helps women understand that eating breakfast, instead of skipping it, can actually help them lose weight more effectively," says Baynes. "When women are tempted by a muffin at 11 AM, Special K provides a sweet choice with its Chocolatey Delight cereal that enables them to indulge and still manage their weight."

Through these constant, useful tips, Special K builds a partnership with its consumers.

"Weight management is a lonely pastime," notes Baynes. "Special K provides a partnership, a community, a forum to help. We are now in the era of managing relationships and building dialogues, not just managing brands."

DIGITAL CHANGES ENABLE DIALOGUE

Like many of the other experts interviewed for this book, Baynes points out the tremendous impact and opportunity presented by digital changes.

"The communications landscape has changed and we are in an interesting evolution," he says. "Marketing used to be brand-to-consumer. Now, with technology and social media, marketing has become more consumer-to-consumer. In the future, I think it will evolve further to consumer-to-brand."

Given the growth in social media and social networking in recent years, Baynes' prediction seems to already be coming true. Women are flocking to Web sites with communities, blogs, and social networking sites. It seems that women's presence in the digital arena will be sustained. A recent study by the Pew Internet & American Life Project revealed that female teens are the primary creators of Web content, far outpacing their male peers in the area of blogging, Web site building, and creating social networking profiles. According to the study, the overall number of teen bloggers doubled between 2004 and 2006, due in large part to girls' participation.[3] With teenage girls producing an increased amount of online content and spending an increased amount of time online, the use of the digital world to facilitate a dialogue with women holds true now and looks to be even more prominent in the future of marketing to women.

Use of the Web by women and girls enables them to access opinions, recommendations, and information in a way that is faster and easier than ever before. In essence, those Web connections are becoming like family and friends to female consumers. Both qualitative and quantitative research shows that family and friends are now the most credible sources of information for female consumers, surpassing experts, Web sites, and advertising. Those friends and family who are so influential in a woman's purchasing life can now be online, as well as offline, in-person relationships.

"A recommendation from a friend scores way above traditional broadcast communications mediums as a driver of purchase intent," Baynes observes.

> That intuitively makes sense for a major purchase like a car or perhaps a camera. We wondered, though, if that holds true for a category like cereal. What we found was that if you are addressing an important need-state, like weight management, friends and family are still very relevant. It's something they want to talk about. Word of mouth is, indeed, as relevant for a weight-management cereal line as it is for an expensive purchase.

For those of you wondering if word-of-mouth marketing is relevant to your brand or business, I would encourage you to explore it. Clearly, your brand must have a real role to play in addressing a key need-state or core anxiety. If it does not, you may need to make product changes before thinking about the marketing. If it does, then getting your consumers to talk to each other could be a valuable tool in building credibility for your brand or business.

GO AHEAD . . . LOSE CONTROL

Getting consumers to talk also implies a loss of control over the brand. As the patterns of control change, the marketing must also change.

"I hear marketers complain that they are losing control. That should not be a bad thing. The really good marketers say 'fantastic.' They see the opportunity to really listen and then apply that listening to make changes," says Baynes. "Smart marketers will use the environment to their advantage against their competition. It's not a one-dimensional environment anymore."

While losing control implies high risk, it is not losing control that is the real risk. Businesses that fail to truly engage consumers in brand management will begin to lose traction in comparison with those that do work hand-in-hand with women. A partnership with female consumers requires listening, asking questions, and—the big challenge—changing.

Additionally, it is not a mass communications environment anymore. A number of experts who I interviewed talked about the need to develop real, one-on-one relationships with women. Women themselves, with little time for commercial messages, are driving a change to more personalized communications.

"Women are asking, 'why do I want to listen to that brand?' There should not be broad demographics with broad shotgun marketing approaches," Baynes points out. "Brands need to know who their most relevant consumer is. That's why strategy will rise to the top of the marketing agenda, not just good execution. What marketers don't do is as important as what they do."

Baynes cites Kashi, a natural food line owned by Kellogg Company that positions itself as "seven whole grains on a mission," as a great example of a brand that not only has developed one-on-one relationships with its consumers but also has converted those relationships into advocacy.

"They know who their most valuable consumers are and it's not everyone," Baynes observes. "In the absence of a mass-market approach, the brand has achieved a great scale of growth. It can be done."

RELATIONSHIPS TRUMP BRAND MANAGEMENT

When I asked Baynes about the one must-do for marketers trying to reach today's multi-minding women, his comments included something to do, as well as something not to do. One of the most renowned marketers in the world today, Baynes advises others to stop just managing brands and to start focusing on relationships.

"When you ask a woman about the characteristics of a good relationship, she will cite qualities like listens well, tolerance, compassion, pleasant surprises, and passion. That's what we have to deliver," explains Baynes. He shares a terrific example:

> Think of a big presentation to a ballroom full of people versus talking one-on-one with someone. The way those two sets of communication take place are completely different. On stage to a mass audience, you are telling. There is not an exchange. You do not really know how your messages have been received. There isn't immediate feedback. In a one-on-one setting, it's a dialogue, a relationship. You listen, ask questions, and adapt. You may not always be right, so you manage through disagreement. It creates a whole new level of authenticity. These are the dynamics of our current marketing environment. The dialogue, not the presentation, is what we need to focus on.

Building such relationships takes credibility, commitment over time, consistency, and flexibility.

"We may need daily marketing plans instead of yearly marketing calendars," remarks Baynes. "We want to give our consumers reasons every day to go beyond awareness and be advocates—to believe themselves and to pass it on to others. That takes daily work and attention."

Many marketers comment on the challenges of building relationships and advocacy, citing the time and expense it takes compared with mass communications. Baynes, however, challenges that logic:

> If you unlock insights, you will build better connections with consumers, the most valuable consumers, and you will see growth because of it. We can't market with historically proven tactics. The rule book has not yet been written for this environment and we must experiment and learn. Our learning agenda must be as well thought through as our marketing plans. If not, our marketing becomes too mechanical and much less effective.

Special K and Dove are exceptional examples of engaging a holistic, E-surround Programming method for marketing to women. While not every business or brand has the budgets associated with those megabrand efforts, any brand or business can and should put effort into something both Special K and Dove did extremely well—unearthing consumer insights.

One business, which is not a megabrand with millions of marketing dollars to spend, has done a terrific job of both unearthing insights and communicating holistically in the small business arena. The marketing is both sophisticated and simple, and it provides a relevant example if you are a small business owner.

The Izzazu International Salon was launched seven years ago in Pittsburgh, Pennsylvania. Primarily a hair salon, the business has grown steadily and successfully, and now includes a line of hair- and skin-care products as well as plans for location expansion. One of the owners of Izzazu, Emilio Cornacchione, spoke with me about some of the interesting ways the salon is marketing to its primary customer, women.

When considering E-surround Programming (equals, editors, experts, and entertainment), Izzazu effectively taps all four of those credible sources of information. The salon does not spend gobs of money on marketing. Rather, the owners have engaged the four most credible types of sources in smart, focused ways—ways that any business could but that many do not.

Let us look first at entertainment. In the hair style and hair care business, celebrities are often the bellwethers for hot trends. Without the assistance of an agency, the salon owners network with celebrities in some interesting ways.

For example, Izzazu provided IZ brand product samples for the Grammy gift bags. "When celebrities are in Pittsburgh filming movies, Izzazu provides product samples and offers to do their hair and make-up," says Cornacchione.

For the Sundance Film Festival, Izzazu sent product samples to celebrities who had a Pittsburgh connection or had filmed in Pittsburgh.

"The samples are accompanied by a handwritten note from me," he adds. "I get thank you notes and the gesture seems to be genuinely appreciated." The appreciation also translates into celebrity endorsements and coverage, like when Catherine Hickland of the daytime show *One Life to Live* rated an Izzazu hair spray as "off the charts" in a national magazine.

The salon owners and their products have also been marketed through the Home Shopping Network (HSN), enabling exposure to millions of women and providing access to the product that simply is not available through a single, physical location. The HSN appearances positioned the salon owners as national experts and translated into brand-building on a national scope. Local customers appreciate the cachet associated with the owners as nationally acclaimed experts and feel like they can tap into nationally known products in their hometown. The line, called IZ Brand Products, is easy to remember and part and parcel of the salon's name, Izzazu. "It IZ what it IZ" serves as the memorable tagline.

Questions Every Marketer or Business Owner Should Ask

- Which sources of information are most credible to my core audience? Am I engaging those sources as conduits for my brand or business?

- Am I engaging multiple channels and touch points to communicate with my multi-minding audience?

- Is the topic of word-of-mouth marketing or getting family and friends talking at least on my learning agenda, if not already in practice?

- Am I listening to my core consumer, engaging in a dialogue with her and making changes as a result of the input?

- Am I providing rich and robust content about need states or core anxieties to my consumer?

- Am I facilitating consumer involvement in the brand and enabling consumers to take more control?

- Am I reaching her when she is most receptive to my marketing messages?

Also in the realm of experts, Izzazu is testing a new closed-circuit television technology in its salon called "i-vu." With video screens located at each station, women can view a hair style channel and celebrity news channel. More content, including food and education topics, are in the works.

"We are among the first to pick up this technology and so far are getting a great response to the i-vu set-up," notes Cornacchione. "It presents a benefit to our customers and great marketing opportunities. In a salon, a woman tends to relax and is ready to take in information around her. Through this system, we can provide women with useful information and add marketing messages that they seem to be willing to pay attention to."

I think it is an intriguing concept. Closed-circuit television is not new, but you often find it in places, like a hospital or doctor's office, when you have much more important things on your mind. In the case of a salon, I believe Cornacchione is right. Women tend to be more relaxed, doing less multi-minding, and it may be a rare and good time to reach them.

Imagine if you coupled an appropriate marketing message for a cosmetic product that appeared on i-vu and then conducted product sampling to the hair stylists. It could create a comfortable and genuine interaction about a product that is of interest to both parties. Given that hairdressers often are considered experts in applicable categories, your product or service would gain exposure and endorsement from a trusted source. Not only that, but you are reaching a woman at a time of optimal receptivity about certain topics, like beauty. It is a great one-two punch for combating multi-minding.

Beauty opinions are often swayed by editors. At Izzazu, editorial coverage has been generated by creating news for editors to cover. For example, a special and splashy red carpet party was held at the salon in conjunction with the Oscars, driving media coverage and customer attention. The salon routinely pitches the local and national media on items of interest or news, and showcases the earned media, or publicity, in the salon.

With the opening of their new location in the works, the salon owners have some great plans for leveraging the fourth "e" in E-surround—that is, equals or word of mouth. An interesting consumer insight underpins the emerging peer strategy.

"Hip suburbanites are key to the word of mouth for our expansion plans," shares Cornacchione.

> We define hip suburbanites as women who are "raving fans" and who come into the downtown salon from the targeted suburb on a very regular basis. They have a personal relationship with the stylist and that connection keeps them coming back. To the raving fans, we'll add local media and people who are leading business owners in the suburb where we'll open the new salon. We plan to identify about 20 of these people for our "ambassadors program," and engage them from the beginning to get their opinions and feedback. These ambassadors are usually leader-type people with lots of friends. The word of mouth will spread.

Proving they know their audience really well, the owners have started opening the salon on Sundays. "We offer Sunday hours, free parking, 10 percent off all products, and the husbands can watch the kids while mom escapes for a few hours," Cornacchione says. "It's not just our customers who have appreciated the Sunday hours. Our stylists, many of them moms themselves, like the option of working on Sunday when they can have their husbands at home with the kids rather than a sitter. It's been good all-around."

Even with a lean marketing budget, Izzazu and its owners have managed to generate credibility, create branded, quick-connect messaging (it IZ what it IZ), create E-surround Programming, and consistently communicate over time with their audience. That case should give every business owner and brand the inspiration to start doing a better job of communicating with women.

As proven with Special K, Dove, and the local case, Izzazu, consumer insights are at the heart of the marketing. They are highly relevant to the consumers' lives and drive an authentic connection between the brands and their female consumers.

Then, those insights are used holistically in programming with equals, experts, editors, and entertainment. Online forums enable women to talk with other women. Category experts reinforce your efforts and serve as credible messengers. Editorial media coverage drives credible message delivery. Entertainment via sports sponsorships, movie or television placement, and celebrity spokespeople embeds your product into popular culture, an influential medium in women's lives today. With the right insights, you, too, can create holistic marketing-to-women programs on a scale that makes sense for your business.

M^2 Must-Dos

✓ Use a holistic approach in marketing to multi-minding women.
✓ Consider leveraging the most credible sources of information for women, including equals (or peers), experts (will differ by category), editors, and entertainment (or popular culture).
✓ Provide a forum in which real women, who are your target consumers, can talk with each other about the brand and the core need or anxiety that it addresses.
✓ Provide practical tips and tools and convenient access to your brand or service.
✓ Concentrate on a core, target audience that represents the highest strategic value to your brand.
✓ Focus on consumer relationships, not just managing a brand.

Chapter Thirteen

She Is Looking for a Commitment: Consistent Confirmation

In the world of multi-minding, a consistent flow of information is an absolute necessity so that your product or brand is available when a female consumer is ready to research and buy. If you are not consistent, she will miss you.

"With so much to do each day, taking care of my family, working, paying bills, making meals, and running errands, I don't have nearly as much time as I would like to keep up on news and seek out tips and information that are of interest to me," says Joyce, a style-conscious mom in her early 40s.

> Even though I can't read every one, I love the DailyCandy e-mails that appear in my inbox each morning. I feel like I can stay up on trends and new products for my kids, my husband, and for myself. Plus, many of my friends get the daily e-mails, too. They are often a topic of conversation.

After an entire book spent telling marketers how busy women are multi-tasking and multi-minding, it may seem contradictory to point out that women actually do want an ongoing flow of information. But a steady stream of information is valuable to achieving credibility with women. Without such consistent exposure to your products or services, multi-minding women will undoubtedly miss your messages. I call this "Consistent Confirmation."

DRIVEN TO DISTRACTION

Marketers must use Consistent Confirmation as part of a holistic campaign to reach multi-minding female consumers, who simply cannot and will not give you their attention. The seminal research on multi-minding proves that women 25 to 54 are easily distracted. In fact, 4 out of 10 say they have to read or hear something more than once because they get distracted. That equates to 39 percent, which is 8 percent higher than the total public, and 13 percent higher than their male counterparts.[1]

According to that same research, women 25 to 54 are more likely to admit that many thoughts and activities are competing for their attention, making consistent communication even more critical. Seventy-four percent of these women agree that many things are simultaneously competing for their attention. That number is 14 percent higher than women in general, 21 percent higher than the total public, 23 percent higher than men 25 to 54, and 32 percent higher than men in general.

Half of all Americans and men 25 to 54 say they wish they had more time in the day to think, while 65 percent of women in that age bracket agree. What these women really want is more time to accomplish tasks, with 76 percent wishing there were more hours in the day to get things done. Therefore, helping them save time and providing time-sensitive solutions are relevant and well-received strategies.

Six out of 10 women 25 to 54 say they constantly feel like they are being pulled in different directions. Almost 70 percent of the women interviewed agreed with this statement, while just 36 percent of the men reported feeling this way. It is no wonder then that women's attention is frequently distracted and that, as a marketer, you will need to go back to her again and again.

IS EVERY DAY TOO MUCH?

DailyCandy, the example mentioned at the beginning of this chapter, is the epitome of Consistent Confirmation. A free daily e-mail "from the front lines of fashion, food, and fun," DailyCandy provides those who sign up with the scoop on "hot new restaurants, designers, secret nooks, and charming diversions in your city and beyond." Is Daily-Candy too much on a daily basis? Not according to its millions of dedicated readers.

DailyCandy is a brand that is welcomed into the inboxes of multi-minding women, because it provides relevant tidbits of information with links to more in-depth information on topics that are relevant to women. The information provided is deemed to have gone through the credible filter of the DailyCandy, which is trend information you can use.

Consistent Confirmation is a cornerstone in effectively reaching your female consumers. It is important for another big and important reason, as well. Every satisfied female customer becomes a highly credible ambassador for your brand. Remember the Wella shampoo commercial from years ago that said, "And she'll tell two friends, and they'll tell two friends and so on and so on"? That same dynamic is alive and well, but at a rapidly accelerated pace due to technology.

Through online communities, Web sites and blogs, average women can now tell thousands of virtual friends what they think with the click of a few keys. As I have said in previous chapters, online communities are the new backyard fence, and conversations about everything, including your brand or business, take place in those communities. Just go to Google.com and Technorati.com and search for your brand or business. If you have not done so, you may be astonished at the level of conversation going on right now. If your brand or business does not appear in those conversation threads, you should be worried. That means you are not part of the conversation at all and since we are approaching the point at which consumers are helping to co-manage brands, your brand or business is close to extinction.

That conversation is fed through Consistent Confirmation activities—small and ongoing communication that keeps your brand alive in the minds of women. I am going to share some good examples later in the chapter. But first, I want to share what I consider to be an excellent and sophisticated example of Consistent Confirmation.

PERSONALIZED CONSISTENT CONFIRMATION GETS RESULTS

Perhaps one of the most extreme examples in which Consistent Confirmation is needed is in higher education. Selecting a college or university is one of the biggest, most expensive, and time-consuming decisions many families will ever make. What I find particularly interesting is that most Consistent Confirmation happens after a purchase, as a way to keep the relationship going and to pave the way for subsequent or increased purchases. In higher education, Consistent Confirmation may need to start years before a decision is actually made.

Attending a college or university is a relatively costly "purchase" and the decision cycle is typically long. It is a complex decision that is researched extensively and made by a team of "consumers," including the student, the parents, other close relatives, and/or those paying the bill.

JoAnne Boyle, Ph.D., and president of Seton Hill University in Greensburg, Pennsylvania, knows the process well. During her tenure, enrollment at the private, Catholic institution has increased dramatically. For much of the university's 90-year history, it was focused on educating women. However, Seton Hill is now a co-ed institution. The history is important here because the vast majority of students who have "purchased" an education at Seton Hill and the resulting alumni base are female.

Boyle offers a number of perceptive thoughts, especially when it comes to Consistent Confirmation, that echo some of the same trends other marketing-to-women thought-leaders in this book have offered.

Mainstream marketers would be wise to adopt some of Seton Hill's approaches, which will be detailed on the next few pages.

"Recruiting students is a very personalized process," Boyle stresses. "We literally recruit students one by one. Mass communication is mostly wasted dollars. We do it for a certain level of awareness, but our results are driven by personalized relationships." Now, there is an example of all of the advice shared by many of the experts in this book wrapped up in action.

MASS PERSONALIZATION?

Of course, that personalized approach is a huge challenge for mass marketers trying to reach tens of millions of female consumers rather than trying to recruit a few hundred students. It is, however, the direction that mass marketers will need to pursue if they are to succeed with women in the future. Many of the experts in this book speak to the importance of developing real relationships with female consumers. Smart use of technology, local market versus solely national efforts, and engagement of key influencers can all be used to successfully personalize marketing while reaching significant numbers of women.

"The one mass communications vehicle that has really netted results in terms of student enrollment is news," notes Boyle. "The recent announcement about our new theater and arts center, which received widespread coverage in the local papers and media, has led directly to doubling enrollment in the programs."

Earlier in the book, I covered the value of editorial media and cited it as one of the most credible sources of information to many women. Seton Hill's public relations efforts for the new theater project have been outstanding and are resulting in tangible business results.

With the exception of public relations, the overall lack of direct results with mass communication has led to tailored initiatives. Seton Hill's marketing effort not only has to be personalized, but also has to span the decision-making process over several years, hence a real need for consistency.

"The decision to select a college becomes serious in a student's junior year in high school," Boyle explains. "Once the PSAT [Preliminary Scholastic Aptitude Test] tests start, the buzz in high schools about college selection begins. That's when we get inquiries."

Those inquiries start the tailored recruitment process. Starting with about 14,000 inquiries, the university then nets approximately 2,000 actual applications.

"We pay a great deal of attention to those students who meet our admissions criteria and who appear serious about wanting to attend Seton Hill," Boyle says.

We assign a personal admissions counselor to highly regarded recruits to ensure there is one consistent point of contact and those counselors are in tune with important events in the lives of prospective students. If one of those students says she's in an important high school theater production, the admissions counselor calls to see how it went. It's a structured process built around showing students and their families that we care because we really do.

What mother, who spends at least 75 percent of her time thinking about her family's needs, or any parent for that matter, would not respond favorably to genuine interest in her child's success? None that I know.

Brands and businesses take note: This business has achieved success, in this case increased enrollment, via tailored communications and focusing on what is relevant to the consumer over time. Imagine what more mainstream brands could achieve if they employed a similar approach scaled to reach millions of women one by one, rather than as a homogenous group.

LOW-TECH, HIGH-TOUCH CONSISTENT CONFIRMATION

Earlier in the chapter, I mentioned how important Consistent Confirmation is to create ambassadors for brands. This concept is especially true with higher education.

"Often times, a prospective student is first introduced to the university by an alum," Boyle notes.

Most often, that alum is a woman who is a mom, aunt, teacher, neighbor, or guidance counselor for the student. Students come to us because of the long-lived relationships we have with important women in their lives. One-half of our freshman class has strong connections with someone who knew the university. We get endorsements from our female alum base every day.

That means that at least one-half of the college's "sales" are generated via women who are happy to serve as unpaid ambassadors for the brand.

"Just a few hours ago, I was in the elevator here at Seton Hill when a 30-something woman said, 'Hi, JoAnne. I am a graduate and today I've brought one of my students and her parents to look at the university,'" relates Boyle. "It's very common for prospective students to come to us because an alum—a mother, aunt, teacher, or neighbor—attended Seton Hill and that alum brings the student for a visit here. It's a powerful endorsement and one that happens frequently without us even orchestrating it."

The university's Consistent Confirmation has a life of its own. The combination of credibility from the alumni and consistency of the activity is powerful, all in the hands of the "consumers." Most businesses or brands would swoon over that level of consumer engagement.

TECHNOLOGY AIDS CONSISTENCY

Boyle predicts that the future of marketing for colleges and universities will be, not unlike many other areas, driven by technology.

"Recruitment, applications, campus visits, and personal relationships will all be online," speculates Boyle. "Life is taking place online for many of our students. They are completely tech-native and in a few years, their parents will be, too."

Another trend that Boyle has spotted, also enabled by technology, is the extended influence of high school friends.

"With every student now equipped with at least one cell phone, computers, and mobile devices, there is continuity with friends from high school that was just not possible before," she notes.

That could be an important development for marketing-to-women marketers to pay attention to over time. The power of word of mouth and influence among high school friends could now last a lifetime and could be a powerful network to tap.

CONSISTENT CONFIRMATION IN ACTION

DailyCandy and Seton Hill University provide thorough and long-term examples of Consistent Confirmation. I have collected a number of other good online and offline examples, as well, which I will share as they may be easy ways to begin Consistent Confirmation for your brand or business.

ONLINE EXAMPLES OF CONSISTENT CONFIRMATION

Research conducted by the Canned Food Alliance (CFA) revealed that most women still do not know what they will make for dinner on a given night even at 4:00 PM. With that insight in hand, the CFA devised dinnertime e-mails. These e-mails, which provide quick, easy, and nutritious dinner recipes, are sent each week to a database of subscribers. The brilliant part is that the recipes are sent mid-afternoon, just when most women are starting to think about what they will make for dinner. The e-mails provide a just-in-time solution for women linked to a call to action to buy canned products. These weekly e-mails provide year-round Consistent Confirmation. That is a win-win effort.

Amazon.com does a nice job of Consistent Confirmation through its "if you liked that book, then you'll like this one" e-mails. Having recently purchased a book on Amazon about working moms, I received an e-mail with several book selections on similar topics. Surmising my interests based on purchasing behavior, Amazon did my homework for me. I like that because I did not have to think about my next book choice, and it saves me time. Of course, it also keeps Amazon at the top of my mind, which is okay with me because I frequently purchase books on Amazon. When consumers are engaged with a brand, such push e-mails are relatively inexpensive ways to create Consistent Confirmation with a brand.

Some online retailers, like Land's End, will automatically provide return mailing labels when they send you the item you have ordered. I have heard women comment that they will order only from e-tailers who provide those labels since returns are so common. Women do not want to waste time searching for return addresses and packaging. It is a hassle. Companies that provide this convenience show they understand the hassle and are willing to help. It is a simple act that reaffirms a woman is doing business with someone who understands her and is acting on this understanding. It also drives repeat purchases.

Several companies I know have started consumer panels—or groups of women in the target audience with which the company engages on a regular basis—for input, comments, and new product previewing. Panels are great tools to consistently reinforce with a key customer base the notion that they are important enough to be consulted. Panels can be conducted online or in person, although the online forum makes sense most of the time from a cost standpoint. Again, the key is to act on the input and feedback. If no action is taken as a result of the input, women will opt out and you will end up creating brand enemies.

Remember, women will tell friends—online and offline—about their good and bad panel experiences, so what happens with the panel does not stay with the panel. That is, in fact, the way you want it to work as women then become peer-to-peer ambassadors for your brand or business.

Reminders are another online tool that can be leveraged for Consistent Confirmation. If you are willing to part with a little personal information about the dates of birthdays in your family, online party supply retailers like Birthday Express will send you information timed in advance of your family members' birthdays. They do the thinking for you and provide a reminder, which is often needed with multi-minding women.

OFFLINE EXAMPLES OF CONSISTENT CONFIRMATION

Using technology and online methods is a quick and cost-efficient way to consistently communicate with your female consumers, but there are other options. Connecting with consumers via phone, in person, or in

---

Questions Every Marketer or Business Owner Should Ask

- Do I have a method of Consistent Confirmation that enables my product or business to live on in the minds of my female consumers?

- What helpful and relevant role can my brand or business play in the daily lives of my consumers?

- Have I asked my core consumers to serve as ambassadors in some way for my brand or business? What incentive do they have for doing so?

- Am I engaged in personalized communications rather than just a mass approach? How am I delivering personalized communications to my core consumers or prospective consumers?

- Am I using technology to enable cost-effective mass personalization?

---

other tangible ways can provide the right dose of personal touch (that is, high-touch confirmation).

Another way to ensure that a brand experience thrives is through postpurchase surveys. Such surveys usually make more sense for large purchases or services rather than everyday items. Surveys can be conducted online or via phone. If you really are interested in customer feedback from a woman, having a person on the phone is better proof of your interest than an automated call.

The key to obtaining feedback is to create an expectation that you will do something with that feedback. If you do not prove you have done something with the feedback, you have wasted a woman's valuable time and she will not waste her time again. In fact, you very likely have just lost a customer. My car dealer does such surveys, and at first, I appreciated that the company promptly followed up to hear about my satisfaction. After several years, however, the service is still lacking and I no longer bother to answer the follow-up calls. I am convinced it is of no use and will buy my next car somewhere else.

Here is an example in a different category, travel and leisure. Just like in many other categories, women are making the majority of the decisions when it comes to family vacations. Having rented beach homes in the Outer Banks for many years, I have seen a number of good examples of Consistent Confirmation. To rent such a home, you must make reservations almost a year before your stay and all rent is due months before you arrive. Therefore, the actual purchase is made well in advance. The owners of the home that we currently rent do two things, in particular, that make us realize we have made a good decision.

Upon arrival at the home, we find a basket full of enough food to prepare one hearty Italian meal, along with a nice bottle of wine. It also includes a welcome note. After a long trip, going straight to the grocery store for supplies, which is usually the woman's responsibility, is a pain. You are trying to unload the car, let the kids run free, and settle in. The basket enables the family to enjoy a nice meal and mom does not have to run right to the grocery store. Thank you. Now, please do not take this away, because I have come to count on that meal being there for me and my family!

The owners also provide more personalized follow-up. In the middle of the week, they call to introduce themselves. They ask how we are enjoying our time and if the house is meeting our needs. They ask whether there is anything they can do or equip the house with that would make our stay even better. Now, our connection is not just with a beach rental house, but with real people who seem to show genuine interest in our enjoyment. But note, they call only once. More frequent calls would seem like they are checking up on us, not nicely checking in. It is no surprise that, because we feel so welcome, we love to rent that particular house.

Another travel example is hotels. As a frequent traveler, I have had and heard of many experiences both good and bad. Most times, consumers make a reservation when planning a hotel stay. The purchase of the hotel room is made in advance. There are great opportunities to reaffirm a hotel choice and to tap into the power of recommendation through how consumers are treated when they check in and out. Many of my female business colleagues like to stay at hotels that remember them by name and welcome them back when they arrive. Those gestures make people, especially women, feel comfortable. That recognition and greeting will more effectively reach women than a costly television advertising campaign. You would think every hotel would do it, but they do not.

Simple things like a personal touch and kind words are powerful tools in reinforcing a purchasing decision and creating brand ambassadors. The women who are making 85 percent of the household decisions are becoming increasingly responsible for business-to-business spending. Most people appreciate a nice greeting, a kind "thank you," and acknowledgment of them by name if they are a repeat customer.

When I go to the little boutique shoe store in my town, I am greeted by name and asked how my kids are. When I go to the shoe store at the airport, where I have purchased many pairs of shoes over the years, I am greeted with a standard "What can I help you find today?" I prefer to spend my money at the boutique in town because I get confirmation that I am an important customer based on the personal touch. I also recommend the local store to my family and friends.

Consistent Confirmation is an essential component in a holistic marketing campaign aimed at women. Multi-minding women simply do not have the time to catch all of the messages a marketer launches into the marketplace, so a consistent flow of messages is absolutely necessary to reach her. Both online and offline formats can provide ways to consistently and cost-effectively reach your female consumer.

When I asked Boyle what one thing she would recommend to marketers as they try to reach multi-minding women, she referenced something she and her team do extremely well.

"The more you can personalize your efforts, the better," she insists. "We have learned the lesson that personalized relationships net results." That advice is one of the central themes I have heard from experts interviewed for this book and I could not agree more.

M^2 Must-Dos

✓ Engage a community of women online so that your site is a forum for a broader discussion on related topics that are important to your audience.

✓ Think about high-tech and high-touch methods for creating consistency in communicating to women.

✓ Engage those women who have purchased your product in the past to become product ambassadors with their peers.

✓ Consider online tools and e-mails to create simple, cost-effective consistency.

Chapter Fourteen

What Does the Future Hold? Multi-Minders Becoming Co-Brand Managers

Get ready for the next women's liberation movement. With everything on a multi-minder's mind, you would think she already has enough to keep her busy. In the future, though, I predict that female consumers will actually take on an increasing role with brands and businesses. Based on the interviews in this book, my observations, and my conversations with many women, I think women will be co-managing brands along with the individuals who have the official titles of brand manager, small business owner, or marketing director. This partnership will exist with the brands that dare to let go and share the steering wheel with their consumers. Sound implausible? Read on.

Average people are more connected and more in control of communications than they have ever been at any other time in history. Technology of all types has enabled our super-connectivity. With the press of a button, one person can start a sea change in a positive or negative direction. Brand fans can quickly and easily share their good feelings, but bad experiences also can be posted immediately and travel like wildfire.

Look at the rise and growth of social networking sites. According to the results of a ComScore study regarding the global reach of major social networks, such sites are growing rapidly, ranging from 72 percent for MySpace to a 172 percent growth rate for Bebo, and a 270 percent increase for Facebook. ComScore notes that this global growth means that online social networking is not a fad, but a larger expression of a global Internet culture that is becoming more integrated every year.[1] Where once there may have been a desire to connect, there is now that same desire coupled with tools that enable that connectivity.

The Internet has also enabled everyday consumers to become more involved in business than ever before.

"Ordinary people are making your business their business as democratized media and information have made corporations more accessible—and accountable," notes a recent article in *Advertising Age* magazine.[2] The article continues,

> Anyone with Internet access can find out just about anything they want about your company online, a platform that also allows consumers to "talk back" to big businesses through blogs, message boards, product reviews, and the like … CMOs [chief marketing officers] need to be actively engaged in those conversations.

Media coverage abounds on the topic of consumer connectivity and the potential power those consumers will possess. *BRANDWEEK* magazine's Outlook for 2008 issue featured the headline "Consumers Are Winning. Any Ideas?" The article says consumers have more tools at their disposal than ever and that they are "winning the arms race against advertisers."[3]

In the *Wall Street Journal*'s "Thinking about Tomorrow" special report, experts speculate that "technology will continue to transform the rituals of everyday life."[4] In the "How We Shop" section of that same report, almost all of the content focuses on online shopping and how it will become much more personalized.

Yahoo! recently launched Shine, a new site for women 25 to 54, citing this group as a key demographic that was underserved until this time. Yahoo! officials said the move was in response to advertisers in a number of categories, ranging from consumer-packaged goods to retail, who have requested more ways to reach female consumers.

According to a spokesperson for Yahoo!, "These women were sort of caretakers for everybody in their lives. They didn't feel like there was a place that was looking at the whole them—as a parent, as a spouse, as a daughter. They were looking for one place that gave them everything." Because of the growing popularity of blogs with women, Shine will be presented in a blog form (at http://shine.yahoo.com) with commentary from an editor.

EXPERTS PREDICT CONSUMER CONTROL

Beyond the statistics, media coverage, and significant marketplace developments, I look to the telling comments of experts quoted throughout this book:

Mark Baynes, global chief marketing officer at Kellogg's notes,

> The communications landscape has changed. We are in an interesting evolution. Marketing used to be brand-to-consumer. Now, with technology and social media, marketing has become

more consumer-to-consumer. In the future, I think it will evolve further to consumer-to-brand.

Mimi Doe, parenting guru and noted author, believes, "Women want to be more invested than ever in their choices, so give them a reason to be invested."

Hedy Lukas, vice president of integrated marketing at Kimberly-Clark, adds, "Today, women are not relying on governments or big organizations to make changes when it comes to making this world a better place. They see it as a personal responsibility."

Gay Browne, founder of Greenopia.com, will begin to harness consumer feedback on green topics and products, and then make that information available to all via Web site ratings.

One of the most important figures in the entire world of consumer marketing, A. G. Lafley, chief executive officer of Procter & Gamble and co-author of *The Game-Changer* (2008), acknowledges the rising power of the consumer. In a *Fortune* magazine interview for the America's Most Admired Companies issue, he notes,

> We put the consumer at the center of everything we do. Three billion times a day, P&G brands touch the lives of people around the world. Our goal is to delight consumers at two moments of truth: first, when they buy a product and, second, when they use it. To achieve that, we live with our consumers and try to see the world and opportunities for new products through their eyes. At P&G, the CEO is not the boss—the consumer is. In ways large and small, we were not living up to the "consumer is boss" standard and we were paying for that lapse.[5]

It seems that many sources are pointing in the direction that increasing consumer involvement will be a natural evolution of the marketing process. Just like relationships in real life take time to build, it also takes time and effort to build a trusting relationship with consumers. The traditional brand-management system, which assigns brand managers to a brand for 12 to 18 months, does not seem to have a vested stake in long-term relationships with consumers. In that case, relationship-building can be institutionalized through communications agencies (advertising and public relations, usually) that stay with a brand longer than the average brand manager. The agencies should be steeped personally in the female consumer audience, rather than just reading research.

MARKETING TO WOMEN IS NOT JUST A JOB

I know a number of clients and agency professionals who continually educate themselves about the digital landscape, marketing trends, and the marketing-to-women area. Many of these professionals are women who not only have a passion for those areas, but also live the life of the women and moms that represent lucrative target audiences. They are immersed in their professional and personal lives as women in the marketplace.

One such woman is Dale Bornstein, partner and director of global practices at Ketchum, a global public relations firm. Another such woman is Janet Riccio, executive vice president at the giant communications holding company, Omnicom. She is also the leader of G23, Omnicom's strategic women-focused consultancy, which comprises senior female communications leaders. Riccio provides some fascinating and insightful thoughts on the future of marketing to women that serve as ideal fodder for the conclusion of this book and the ongoing journey in marketing to women.

Bornstein is a colleague of mine, a true leader in the agency business, as well as a devoted wife and mother. She and I have talked at length about the future role of female consumers. She has always been one of those people who has a keen sense of the future because she is a keen watcher of trends. Her thoughts about women and how they will move into roles as co-managers of brands are worth sharing and provide a good deal of insight.

"Consumers no longer have to take what the marketplace gives them," notes Bornstein.

> Consumers, especially moms, now have a voice and they are exerting it. Never before has there been a need for brands and businesses to be so relevant. Smart brands are recognizing the power of female consumers in the marketplace in terms of the power of their purses and the power of their voices.

Just take a look at the explosion of mommy sites and blogs as a prime indicator of Bornstein's point. From the highly trafficked sites like Clubmom.com and Cafemoms.com to growing sites like Coolmompicks.com and Mommytrackd.com, women are expressing their viewpoints on everything from pregnancy to politics and on every product imaginable. They will tell a marketer or business owner anything they want to know.

"It used to be in the classic model of marketing, that marketers took really good guesses," says Bornstein. "They conducted research. They did focus groups and then tested *their* hypothesis. Now, the twist is that brands need to do enough homework to be highly relevant by listening, really listening, to the right consumers and enough *consumer* voices that products are actually developed and marketed in conjunction with the consumer."

Those voices are more accessible than ever before and they now expect marketers to listen. Whether you like it or not, women are taking control of brands and businesses that mean something to them. That phenomenon inherently implies that brand managers and business owners are losing a significant degree of control.

FIND YOUR WAY BY LOSING CONTROL

Based on Bornstein's comments and those of many other thought-leaders in this book, not only is losing some control of your brand good, but it also is inevitable if your brand or business is to succeed in the future. Consumer voices and participation can add insights to product development, marketing, and product advocacy. Moms are an audience that Bornstein sees as particularly important when it comes to brand engagement.

"Moms want products that help them and make them feel good. Family, health of the family, and the health and well-being of the community are three key motivators," Bornstein says.

How can a brand know what's going on in the minds of these consumers unless these consumers are involved in the brand, starting at product development through consumer communications? Brands belong in the hands of consumers, not in warehouses. By sharing control, brands become more relevant. Brands should actively seek consumer ownership.

A number of brands already are sharing control of many facets of their products with female consumers. Baby gear manufacturers, for example, seem to be listening to and engaging women more than ever. The available models now meet a variety of needs versus the handful of standard items that were marketed just five years ago. Strollers used to be bulky, be hard to handle, and come in such desirable color choices as navy and gray. Now, thanks to input from women in product development, strollers can be found for a wide variety of needs, such as for jogging and navigating city streets, or they may be ultra-light. Colors and fabric patterns now run the gamut, including animal prints and trendy palettes.

One particular baby products company, 4Moms, leverages the insights literally from four moms who have a combined total of 13 children. The company produces products like an infant tub that delivers real innovation in terms of meeting unmet needs identified by moms and technical experts. In the case of the tub, clean and warm water was the unmet need, which was solved by using a new tub design and digital temperature gauge.

Food companies are engaging panels of real women and moms or tapping experts to better understand what women really want and need. Libby's canned vegetables, for example, is engaging a mom expert to help devise and communicate ways to bring families back to the dinner table while stretching the consumers' food dollar and delivering quick and nutritious meals. With that program, Libby's is providing a triple benefit to moms. What multi-minding mom could resist?

An article in *PRWeek*, a public relations industry trade magazine, featured a story that stated, "An unusual experiment in relinquishing brand control pays off for IKEA." A brand fan and blogger, named IKEA Jen, connected comedian and filmmaker Mark Malkoff to IKEA and its public relations department. Malkoff is known for his other publicized activities, such as patronizing all of Manhattan's 171 Starbuck's franchises in one day.

After a series of discussions, Malkoff moved in to the IKEA store in Paramus, New Jersey, and lived there from January 7–12, 2007, with access to all areas. The 24 short videos that resulted from his stay were posted on Marklivesinikea.com. The videos attracted more than 15 million viewers, 9 million of whom visited the site in the first week.

"This was the most successful public relations campaign in the United States and the largest media coverage for any campaign," says Marty Marston, commercial public relations manager for IKEA.[6] This leap of faith to cede control of its brand, considered in the past to be a reasonable risk, proved successful in terms of awareness, media coverage, and consumer engagement.

Relinquishing control to consumers may not be an easy decision. Choosing how to turn over that control must be in line with brand essence or corporate culture. Given that consumers, especially women, say family and friends are the most trusted source of information, giving up some control should at least be considered.

MOMPRENEURS RULE, BRANDS DROOL

Many brands have not cultivated the necessary level of involvement, which is one of the big reasons why there are so many mompreneurs today. "These women know what they need and want, and are not waiting around until an established marketer delivers it to them," says Bornstein.

Her comments are already playing out in reality. According to the Center for Women's Business Research, for the past two decades, women-owned firms have continued to grow at approximately two times the rate of all firms. The report goes on to say that women emphasize relationship-building, as well as fact-gathering, and are more likely to consult with experts, employees, and fellow business owners than are men. Interestingly, women business owners are nearly twice as likely as men business owners to intend to pass the business on to a daughter or daughters.[7] If those intentions become a reality, more women than ever will personally take on the responsibility for delivering products to the marketplace, rather than waiting for marketers to listen to and engage them.

Numerous women and moms have created products because they experienced a need and could not find a solution in the marketplace. They rely on their own experiences and insights and those of their family and friends.

Take Robeez shoes, for example. Sandra Wilson, a mom whose job was eliminated in an airline restructuring, was at home with her son, Robert, who was learning to walk. She decided she wanted to spend more time with her son, so she did not go back to work. While at home, she sewed a pair of soft-soled shoes for him and they seemed to help his balance as he learned to walk. Given that insight, she sewed 20 more pairs and took them to a gift show. They sold out and she signed up 15 retailers to sell them. She started making more and the business grew and grew. In 2006, Stride Rite purchased the Robeez business and, today, sales top $15 million.

At the same time that Wilson was building a successful business selling shoes, she also created the Heart and Sole Foundation. She dedicates her time and supports mompreneurs through her blog and her advice. Robeez carries on those traditions.

Look, too, at Sara Blakely, inventor of Spanx footless pantyhose. Blakely came up with Spanx control-top hose with an adjustable band along the calf, the perfect solution to the age-old problem of underwear lines under pants and skirts that you want to wear with open-toed shoes or sandals.

"When I went to department stores and boutiques and asked if they had any control-top pantyhose without feet, the answer was always 'no,'" Blakely says. As a result, she invented the solution, single-handedly sold the idea to retailers, and built the business. In the first five months, 50,000 pairs of Spanx pantyhose were sold at $20 each.[8]

"If you can't help her, she may just do it herself," observes Bornstein. "She'll become your competition with built-in focus groups, online communities, and more connectivity than ever before."

This idea is profound for marketers. In essence, not only do women have the insights, but for the first time ever, they also have a relatively effective marketing network at their fingertips.

"More and more moms are looking to intersect motherhood and livelihood. In today's world, that intersection is possible and it could replace some of what mainstream marketers are offering unless they, too, are truly engaged in the female marketplace," Bornstein states.

Women today have the tools and know-how to get what they want, even if it currently is not on the market. If marketers are not listening to them, they will go elsewhere and not necessarily to the traditional competitor. They have the ability, if not engaged in your brand, to do it themselves. Millions of them will do it themselves, and they will erode the market share of many products in the form of a million little razor cuts. Brands and businesses will lose if they are not engaging women and inviting their control now.

WALK IN THE FEMALE SOLE

As the leader of G23, a senior strategic advisory group working with clients who seek more relevant and sustaining connections with women, Janet Riccio believes that women already help marketers tremendously.

"Women give many indicators of what works and what doesn't work for them," says Riccio. "It's a matter of if you are marketing *to* them or partnering *with* them that really matters."

Riccio would know. As an executive vice president at Omnicom, she is in a position to see the best work in communications today in addition to seeing companies that are struggling with their communications to women.

"P&G gets it," she notes. "Some industries are, indeed, headed for a disaster if they refuse to understand women."

"The female sole," is how Riccio describes the manner by which brands or companies should approach their communications. "We need to literally walk in and out of the lives of women and the brands they use to really understand those relationships. It's all based on their relationship with the brand."

The female sole is undoubtedly more challenging to track and monitor these days, especially as those soles are increasingly online.

"Women go online for everything," Riccio says.

What's hot, what's green, what's a good philanthropic cause, it's all found online. Women have always participated strongly in our economy and they have always shared information. With so much activity and commerce online, we now have a participatory economy, one that's based more on exchange than one-way business.

"That dynamic plays directly to the strengths of women, and women are starting to understand how they can leverage their roles and their spending," she added. "Brands will live or die faster than ever before because of the power of women today."

Clearly, this dynamic has significant implications in the external marketplace, many of which have been covered in this book. Women now have the tools at their disposal to transform their inherent

---

Questions Every Marketer or Business Owner Should Ask

- Who are my highest-value consumers?

- How am I marketing *with* those highest-value consumers?

- Am I inviting my female consumers to participate in the co-brand management of my brand or business?

- To what degree is my brand or business comfortable with relinquishing some control of the business to consumers?

- Am I providing ways within my company for women to connect motherhood and livelihood?

- Does my brand have both an offline and online relationship with female consumers?

- Am I on board for the long term in the continuing journey in marketing with women?

---

connectivity into input for brands and to launch new businesses. Companies face significant internal implications, as well.

"It will be increasingly important for women to rise to senior roles in management and politics," Riccio asserts. "Without women at the top, companies will lose to those organizations that do incorporate and value input from women at the highest levels. The female sole must genuinely live within companies for success in the future."

One of the areas that Riccio sees as critical to engaging women is philanthropy. "It's very important to women," she says. So much so that "G23 [the Omnicom consultancy led by and focused on women] will always include recommendations to clients that partner philanthropic along with nonphilanthropic strategies. Corporate and brand philanthropy will play a strong role in the future of marketing with women."

YOUR FUTURE IS IN HER HANDS, HER HOME, HER RELATIONSHIP WITH YOU

In talking about the future of marketing *with* women, as Riccio refers to it, I was especially intrigued by several areas that she mentioned. First, she sees in the not-too-distant future, the challenge of getting "relevant content on all screens." While we are used to thinking of those screens as television or personal computer screens, Riccio's vision includes the mother of all screens, "the flat screen on the refrigerator from which everything will be controlled."

While the technology has been around for a while, it is yet to be fully adopted and utilized by women. In the future, the kitchen will be the command center, complete with technology to power it like never before. Riccio predicts, "Personal organization will take on new heights and present big challenges and opportunities for marketers." Multi-minding women, rejoice. If Riccio is right, more and better tools could be on the way to help make busy lives more manageable.

According to Riccio,

The future success of marketers is firmly in the hands of young women who are in the up-and-coming generations. They are confident in their womanhood and more comfortable than past generations in expressing what being a woman means to them. They are very much individuals and will want marketers to market *with* them, not *to* them.

Riccio still sees a viable role for mass communications in the future when mass awareness is a goal. However, she sees a real movement toward "marketing with the individual and influencer selling":

Women are not a monolithic group. They want marketers to recognize their many roles and to be communicated to in an individualistic and respectful way. We must be more precise in finding consumers who are the most interested in what a brand has to offer. We have to drill down to find the best, multi-dimensional cohort of women for any given product. For example, an audience is not just moms, but perhaps moms who are of color and are nurses that could really be the most valuable to a particular brand.

Women rely on a variety of influencers or credible sources to help them make decisions.

"Bringing the best influencers into the fold for any particular brand will be important and, at the same time, challenging. Influencers are capable of sparking word of mouth, which will continue to be extraordinarily important in reaching women," Riccio stresses. "However, orchestrated word of mouth can come off in a less than authentic way, so constantly refreshing the influencer group and truly providing information to those new influencers can help sustain a more genuine effort."

Given Riccio's keen sense for future trends, I asked her to share one thing she would recommend that marketers must do as they consider their future marketing. "Shift your thinking," she advises. "Forget marketing to women. The word 'to' inherently sounds as though women are not participating, and they are. Partner with them. Don't treat them as one big group of women. Cater to the individual."

There is an old saying that there is no "I" in team. Well, there is a "me" in women. Let them know you are partnering with an individual "me," not just women in general. Perhaps I need to rename this book: *Too Busy to Shop: Marketing with Multi-Minding Me's.*

M^2 Must-Dos

- ✓ Create a partnership with women that will enable them to co-manage your brand or business.
- ✓ Give women compelling reasons to invest in your brand.
- ✓ Create a dialogue with women to get input into everything from unmet needs and product development to marketing and influencers.
- ✓ Consider philanthropic strategies to engage women.
- ✓ Remember that women are a collection of individuals. Find the most relevant "me" in the women you target and market with the me's.
- ✓ Start to study how your brand or business fits into the influential organizational tools that multi-minding women will be using in the not-so-distant future.
- ✓ Become someone who is (or have someone in your company become) truly immersed in the female marketplace.

Notes

CHAPTER ONE

1. Ketchum Global Research Network, Women 25 to 54 Launch Study, December 2005.

2. Marti Barletta, *Marketing to Women: How to Increase Your Share of the World's Largest Market*, 2nd ed. (Chicago: Dearborn Trade Publishing, 2006).

3. Pallavi Gogoi, "I Am Woman, Hear Me Shop," *BusinessWeek* online, February 14, 2005, http://www.businessweek.com/2005/02/14.

4. M2W Conference Web Site, Fast Facts, http://www.m2w.biz/fastfacts.html.

5. M2W Conference Web Site, Fast Facts, http://www.m2w.biz/fastfacts.html.

6. Pallavi Gogoi, "I Am Woman, Hear Me Shop," *BusinessWeek* online, February 14, 2005, http://www.businessweek.com/2005/02/14.

7. Center for Women's Business Research Reports, 2007.

8. Genevieve Bos, "Memo from the Bos," *PINK Magazine*, June/July 2005.

9. Tom Peters and Marti Barletta, *Trends* (New York: Dorling Kindersley, 2005).

10. Mattel, What We Believe, http://www.webelieveingirls.com/what_we_believe (accessed November 5, 2007).

11. Mattel, What We're Doing, http://www.webelieveingirls.com/what_we_believe/what_were_doing.html (accessed November 6, 2005).

12. Mattel, We Believe in Girls Advisory Council, http://www.webelieveingirls.com/what_we_believe/what_were_doing.html (accessed November 6, 2007).

13. Mattel, "Global Media's Coverage of Tween Girls," MME Research Report, March 22, 2007, http://www.webelieveingirls.com/what_we_believe/what_were_doing.html (accessed November 21, 2007).

14. Clifford Krauss, "Harley Woos Female Bikers," *New York Times*, July 25, 2007.

15. Harley-Davidson, "Harley to Woo Women at South Dakota Rally," news release, July 27, 2007.

16. Clifford Krauss, "Harley Woos Female Bikers," *New York Times*, July 25, 2007.

CHAPTER TWO

1. Ketchum Global Research Network, Women 25 to 54 Launch Study, December 2005.

2. Ibid.

3. Ibid.

4. Ibid.
5. The Intelligence Group, Mom Intelligence Report, May 23, 2007.

CHAPTER THREE

1. Bruce Horovitz, "Alpha Moms Leap to Top of Trendsetters," *USA Today*, March 27, 2007.
2. The Intelligence Group, Mom Intelligence Report, May 23, 2007.
3. Stephanie Thompson, "Mommy Blogs: A Marketer's Dream," *Advertising Age*, February 26, 2007.
4. Mark Fitzgerald, "What Do Women Want," *Editor & Publisher*, November 1, 2007.
5. Ketchum Global Research Network, Women 25 to 54 Launch Study, December 2005.
6. Mark Fitzgerald, "What Do Women Want," *Editor & Publisher*, November 1, 2007.
7. Andrea Learned, "The Six Costliest Mistakes You Can Make in Marketing to Women," *Inc.com*, January 2003.
8. Mintel International Group, Marketing to Moms Report, 2007.
9. Sam Ewen, "Lose Control: It's Good for Your Brand," *BRANDWEEK*, November 26, 2007.
10. The Intelligence Group, Mom Intelligence Report, May 23, 2007.

CHAPTER FOUR

1. Yahoo! and Starcom MediaVest Group Research, "Re-Emergence of Daytime Audience," April 2004.
2. Egon Zehnder International, "THE FOCUS" online, *The Egon Zehnder International Leadership Magazine* (accessed August 2, 2007).

CHAPTER FIVE

1. Ketchum Global Research Network, Women 25 to 54 Launch Study, December 2005.
2. Hannah Keeley, *Hannah Keeley's Total Mom Makeover* (Boston: Little, Brown, 2007).
3. Special Advertising Section, *BRANDWEEK*, December 3, 2007.
4. Jack Neff, "CPG Marketers May Have Found Their Mass Vehicle: Search," *Advertising Age*, October 23, 2007.
5. Cable Guide Special Section, *Advertising Age*, May 7, 2007.
6. "Mom Matters," e-newsletter, *Parenting Magazine*, February 2007.
7. Oxygen Network, "Women's Watch: Girls Gone Wired Study," August 2006.

CHAPTER SIX

1. Marti Barletta, *Marketing to Women: How to Increase Your Share of the World's Largest Market*, 2nd ed. (Chicago: Dearborn Trade Publishing, 2006).

CHAPTER SEVEN

1. Ketchum Global Research Network, Women 25 to 54 Study, May 2006.
2. Forrester Research, Inc., "Best Practices, Organic Branding," December 28, 2006.
3. Clair Cain Miller, "The New Back Fence," *Forbes*, April 7, 2008.
4. Jennifer Saranow, "iDo," *Wall Street Journal*, May 3, 2008.
5. Gur Tsabar, "The Googling Mom," *Perspectives*, April 2008.
6. MindShare Research, "Moms Skip Ads on DVRs," May 2008.

CHAPTER EIGHT

1. Ketchum Global Research Network, Women 25 to 54 Study, May 2006.
2. Wikipedia, http://en.wikipedia.org/wiki/Cause_marketing (accessed November 19, 2007).
3. Ibid.
4. Ibid.
5. Cause Marketing Forum, http://www.causemarketingforum.com (accessed November 19, 2007).
6. Cone, Cone Cause Evolution Study, 2007.
7. Ibid.
8. Ibid.; and Cone, Cone Millennial Cause Study, 2006.
9. Ibid.
10. Ketchum Global Research Network, Women 25 to 54 Study, May 2006.
11. Ibid.

CHAPTER NINE

1. "Outlook 2008," *BRANDWEEK*, December 31, 2007.
2. Pallavi Gogoi, "I Am Woman, Hear Me Shop," *BusinessWeek* online, http://www.businessweek.com/2005/02/14, February 14, 2005.
3. Kathy Gerber, "Marketing to Women Special Section," *BRANDWEEK*, December 2007.

CHAPTER TEN

1. Ketchum Global Research Network, Women 25 to 54 Launch Study, December 2005.
2. Ibid.
3. Hartman Group, Marketing to Today's Mom 21st Century Style, May 2006.
4. Kimberley A. Strassel, *Wall Street Journal*, August 31, 2007.
5. Hartman Group, Marketing to Today's Mom 21st Century Style, May 2006.

CHAPTER ELEVEN

1. Ketchum Global Research Network, Women 25 to 54 Launch Survey, 2005.
2. Ibid.

3. Ketchum Global Research Network, Women 25 to 54 Study, May 2006.

4. Ibid.

5. John Rosen and AnnaMaria Turano, *Stopwatch Marketing: Take Charge of the Time When Your Customer Decides to Buy* (New York: Portfolio, 2008).

6. Cheryl Wilbur, "Mom Matters Newsletter, MomConnection Study," *Parenting Magazine*, February 2008.

7. Leslie Sbrocco, *Wine for Women: A Guide to Buying, Pairing, and Sharing Wine* (New York: Morrow, 2003).

CHAPTER TWELVE

1. TNS Media Intelligence/Cymfony, Social Media Study, February 2008.

2. The Intelligence Group, Mom Intelligence Report, May 23, 2007.

3. Pew Internet and American Life Project, Teens and Social Media Study, December 19, 2007.

CHAPTER THIRTEEN

1. Ketchum Global Research Network, Women 25 to 54 Launch Study, 2005.

CHAPTER FOURTEEN

1. comScore, Inc., Report on Worldwide Growth of Selected Social Networking Sites, July 31, 2007.

2. Andrew Bennett, "Consumers Are Watching You," *Advertising Age*, April 7, 2008.

3. "Outlook 2008," *BRANDWEEK*, December 31, 2007.

4. Jessica E. Vascellaro, "The Journal Report: Thinking about Tomorrow," *Wall Street Journal*, January 28, 2008.

5. A. G. Lafley and Ram Charan, "The Consumer Is Boss," *Fortune*, March 10, 2008.

6. Nicole Zerillo, "Home Away from Home," *PRWeek*, April 21, 2008.

7. The Center for Women's Business Research, "Surprising Facts about Women-Owned Businesses Report," March 3, 2008.

8. Jill Westfall, "Leg Work," *MyMidwest Magazine*, March/April 2008.

Bibliography

BOOKS AND MAGAZINES

Bailey, Maria T., and Bonnie W. Ulman. *Trillion Dollar Mom$: Marketing to a New Generation of Mothers*. Chicago: Dearborn Trade Publishing, 2005.

Barletta, Marti. *Marketing to Women: How to Increase Your Share of the World's Largest Market*, 2nd ed. Chicago: Dearborn Trade Publishing, 2006.

Barletta, Marti. *PrimeTime Women: How to Win the Hearts, Minds, and Business of Boomer Big Spenders*. New York: Kaplan, 2007.

BRANDWEEK Magazine. New York: Nielson Business Media.

Brizendine, Louann. *The Female Brain*. New York: Morgan Road Books, 2006.

Doe, Mimi. *Busy but Balanced: Practical and Inspirational Ways to Create a Calmer, Closer Family*. New York: St. Martin's Press, 2001.

Gladwell, Malcolm. *Blink: The Power of Thinking without Thinking*. Boston: Little, Brown, 2005.

Goldstein, Beth. *The Ultimate Small Business Marketing Toolkit*. New York: McGraw-Hill, 2007.

Keeley, Hannah. *Hannah Keeley's Total Mom Makeover*. Boston: Little, Brown, 2007.

Morgan Steiner, Leslie. *Mommy Wars: Stay-at-Home and Career Moms Face Off on Their Choices, Their Lives, Their Families*. New York: Random House, 2006.

Passi, Delia. *Winning the Toughest Customer: The Essential Guide to Selling to Women*. New York: Kaplan, 2006.

PINK Magazine. Atlanta, GA: Pink Street LLC.

Quinlin, Mary Lou. *Time Off for Good Behavior: How Hardworking Women Can Take a Break and Change Their Lives*. New York: Broadway Books, 2005.

Stephens, Nancy. *Customer-Focused Selling: Understanding Customer Needs, Building Trust, and Delivering Solutions . . . the Smarter Path to Sales Success*. Avon, MA: Adams Media, 1998.

Warner, Fara. *The Power of the Purse: How Smart Businesses Are Adapting to the World's Most Important Consumers—Women*. Upper Saddle River, NJ: Pearson Prentice Hall, 2006.

Weiner, Mark. *Unleashing the Power of PR: A Contrarian's Guide to Marketing and Communication*. New York: John Wiley & Sons, 2006.

WEB SITES

CafeMom. www.cafemom.com.
Concepts, Inc. www.coninc.com.
DailyCandy. www.dailycandy.com.
Greenopia. www.greenopia.com.
Hannah Keeley. www.totalmom.com.
Hybrid Mom. www.hybridmom.com.
Ketchum. www.ketchum.com.
Mealtime.org. www.mealtime.org.
Mom Central. www.momcentral.com.
Mommy Track'd LLC. www.mommytrackd.com.
M2Moms. www.m2moms.com.
M2W. www.m2w.biz.
Oxygen Network. www.oxygen.com.
Spiritual Parenting. www.spiritualparenting.com.
Too Busy to Shop. www.toobusytoshop.blogspot.com.
The Trendsight Group. www.trendsight.com.
The Washington Group. www.thewashingtongroup.com.
Zócalo Group. www.zocalogroup.com.

Index

About the Author and Interviewees

Kelley Murray Skoloda is a wife, a mom, a daughter, a sister, an aunt, a good friend to some terrific women, partner/director of Ketchum's Global Brand Marketing Practice, and now an author. She is a recognized authority on marketing to women and is the architect of the widely-publicized Women 25 to 54, a communications offering that presents a better way to reach "multi-minding" female consumers.

In her distinguished career with the global, top-ten public relations firm, Ketchum, she has counseled dozens of companies and blue-chip brands including the American Iron and Steel Institute's Canned Food Alliance, Aetna, GlaxoSmithKline Consumer Healthcare, Daimler Chrysler, Kellogg's Special K and other Kellogg's brands, Kimberly-Clark, Libby's, Rite Aid Corporation, and many others.

Previously, she was the agency's director of business development, working with agency staffers around the world to build new business. She oversaw the implementation of the firm's Customer Relationship Management (CRM) System and activated a global new business network. Kelley holds a certification in Customer-Focused Selling.

Skoloda is a sought-after speaker and commentator on the subject of marketing to women and has been featured in *BusinessWeek Online*, *BRANDWEEK*, *CNNMoney.com*, *Today's Chicago Woman*, *The Washington Post*, *PRWeek*, and others. She was named one of the most influential women in business in the Pittsburgh region by the Pittsburgh Post-Gazette in its "Women at the Helm" special edition. She has also served on the advisory board for *PINK Magazine*. She is filming an episode of a BBC-produced television show called *Beat the Boss*, which is designed to encourage and develop entrepreneurial skills in young people.

Kelley's blog, www.toobusytoshop.blogspot.com, helped to collect input from women for this book. Skoloda earned her MBA from the University of Pittsburgh and her undergraduate degree from Seton Hill University, where she now sits on the Board of Trustees. She and her husband, David, reside near Pittsburgh, Pennsylvania, with their two children, Jake and Ellie.

Marti Barletta, Chief Executive Officer and Founder, TrendSight Group, www.trendsight.com

Marti Barletta is a recognized authority on building marketing, sales, recruiting, and retention results through better communications with women. Author of *Marketing to Women* (2nd edition, January 2006) and co-author with Tom Peters of *Trends* (July 2005), her third book, *PrimeTime Women: How to Win the Hearts, Minds, and Business of Boomer Big Spenders*, was released in January 2007. It features a new focus on the golden bull's-eye of target marketing, PrimeTime Women (women 50 to 70).

Holding a Wharton master's of business administration, she honed her talents via a distinguished career at top-flight agencies like McCann-Erickson, TLK, FCB, and Frankel, and work on blue-chip brands such as Kraft, Kodak, and Allstate. Barletta has been quoted on *CBS Evening News, ABC Money Matters*, and the *Today* show on NBC, as well as in the *Wall Street Journal, New York Times, Fast Company* magazine, *Business Week* magazine, *Entrepreneur* magazine, and many other publications worldwide.

Mark R. Baynes, Global Chief Marketing Officer, Kellogg's, www.kellogg.com

Mark R. Baynes has been global chief marketing officer, Kellogg Company since July 2007. Baynes joined Kellogg's in the United Kingdom in 1990 as senior brand manager and held several positions while in the United Kingdom. He was promoted to marketing manager in 1992; senior marketing manager in 1994; manager, NPD convenience foods in 1996; director, business development in 1997; director, global convenience foods innovation, Kellogg Europe in 1998; and managing director, convenience foods, Kellogg Europe in 1999.

In 2000, Baynes was promoted to vice president, convenience foods innovation, Kellogg USA; in 2002, to vice president, marketing, Morning Foods Division, Kellogg USA; and in 2004, to senior vice president, marketing, Morning Foods Division, Kellogg North America. He was promoted to chief marketing officer, Kellogg North America and global coordinator, Kellogg Company in January 2007.

Baynes received an honors degree in business management from the University of Wessex. Baynes and his wife, Lesley, reside in Hickory Corners, Michigan. They have two children.

Dale Bornstein, Partner/Director, Global Practices, Ketchum, www.ketchum.com

As director of Ketchum's Global Practices, Dale Bornstein is responsible for overseeing the progress, momentum, and growth of the agency's five practices, which include Brand Marketing, Food and Nutrition, Corporate, Healthcare, and Technology. Bornstein is a member of the agency's nine-member Worldwide Executive Committee.

Bornstein has helped shape many of the agency's high-visibility, award-winning initiatives, including a successful viral marketing campaign for Tropicana called www.healthykidshappymoms.com and the launch of WingspanBank.com, the world's first online bank, and its innovative "iboard of directors." Bornstein led Ketchum's Best Teams effort, which included staffers from nearly all of Ketchum's U.S. offices, to successfully conduct media relations and issues management for the 1996 Olympic Torch Relay—an 84-day, 15,000-mile grassroots event that captured the hearts and minds of the American public and the media.

Bornstein received her bachelor of science degree in communication arts from Cornell University, where she graduated with honors.

JoAnne Boyle, President, Seton Hill University, www.setonhill.edu

JoAnne Boyle, Ph.D., has served as the ninth president of Seton Hill University in Greensburg, Pennsylvania, since July 1987. President Boyle has seen the transition of Seton Hill from a women's undergraduate college of about 400 students to a coeducational university with an enrollment of more than 1,800. In addition to baccalaureate degrees in arts, science, and music education, under her leadership the university has added graduate programs leading to a master's degree in nine areas, including business administration, writing/popular fiction, special education, and family therapy.

During Boyle's tenure Seton Hill has strengthened its international programs of faculty and student exchange; established E-Magnify (formerly the National Education Center for Women in Business) and the National Catholic Center for Holocaust Education; opened a tourism and hospitality major with emphasis on the study of the heritage and history of western Pennsylvania; and expanded programs in the natural sciences with an emphasis on undergraduate research on women's health.

Boyle and her husband, Arthur, have 7 children and 13 grandchildren.

Gay Browne, Founder, Greenopia, www.greenopia.com

A lifelong asthmatic, Gay Browne began to search for ways to improve her environment and take better care of herself and her children. She started from the inside out—choosing all-natural alternatives for everything from nutritional habits to bed sheets. In 1994, Browne built the first green home in her Los Angeles' Pacific Palisades community and began the journey that eventually gave rise to the Greenopia guides. In her experience with researching and working with green home developers, interior designers, and furniture dealers, she realized that there was a wealth of green options, but no simple resource to find them. In response,

Browne developed Greenopia to provide a resource to help people like herself make choices to green their lives on a daily basis.

Browne says, "It doesn't have to be all or nothing. Even small changes make a big difference."

Browne currently resides in Santa Barbara, California, with her husband, three children, and three dogs. She continues to make her home as environmentally safe as possible without sacrificing quality, aesthetics, or efficiency.

Kassie Canter, former Chief Communications Officer, Oxygen Network, www.oxygen.com

Kassie Canter is a communications professional with more than 15 years of experience in the field. She has counseled corporate chief executive officers on communications strategies, developed strategic communications campaigns, advised on crisis communications, and overseen advocacy campaigns for many media companies. She served as the chief communications officer at Oxygen Media, where she oversaw all public relations and public affairs activities for the cable network. In addition to determining the company positioning, Canter developed original award-winning campaigns to launch and promote the network's programming. She was the executive producer of an Emmy-nominated public service announcement encouraging women to vote.

Canter holds a bachelor's degree from Tufts University and a master's of public administration from the Kennedy School of Government at Harvard University.

Carol L. Cone, Founder, Cone, www.coneinc.com

Carol L. Cone is nationally recognized for her work in the Cause Branding and strategic philanthropy arenas. As the chair of Cone, she has embraced a steadfast commitment to building substantive and sustainable partnerships between companies and social issues for more than 25 years. Cone has pioneered vibrant new alliances for private-public partnerships to create signature programs for a host of Fortune 500 companies, including the Avon Breast Cancer Crusade, ConAgra Foods' Feeding Children Better Program, PNC's Grow Up Great Program, the American Heart Association's Go Red for Women Program, Reebok's Human Rights Awards, Rockport's Fitness Walking Program, Gillette Women's Cancer Connection, and Polaroid's Project KidCare, among others. Overall, Cone's signature cause programs have raised more than $500 million for various social causes. Today, the Cone firm is acknowledged as the nation's leading Cause Branding consultancy.

Cone is also considered one of the nation's experts in the field and is often solicited by the national media, including *USA Today*, *New York Times*, *Washington Post*, *Los Angeles Times*, *BusinessWeek* magazine, and *Harvard Business Review*.

Emilio Cornacchione, Partner, Izzazu International Salon, www. izzazu.com

With more than 20 years in the beauty industry, Emilio Cornacchione has vast knowledge and experience in various areas of the hair care industry. His expertise ranges from salon customer service to key hairstyling positions for television sitcoms, theater, and fashion shows.

Cornacchione studied at Vidal Sassoon Academy in Los Angeles and the L'Oreal International Institute and is requested by local celebrities and for photo shoots. He has been involved with Hollywood and the theater as well as various assignments with the Pittsburgh Film Office. He is an expert at cutting hair, coloring, and styling. He travels nationally and internationally lecturing and educating on up-and-coming styles and trends.

In its seventh year, Izzazu International Salon has seen many monumental occasions, including the launch of the product line "IZ", being featured on the Home Shopping Network. The city of Pittsburgh recently recognized the salon with an official Izzazu day.

Denis Darragh, General Manager, Forbo Flooring Systems, North America and Asia, www.forbo.com

Denis Darragh is the General Manager of Forbo Flooring Systems in North and Central America and the Asia Pacific Regions. Forbo is the third-largest resilient flooring manufacturer in the world and has been the leader in sustainability initiatives for decades. A graduate of the University of Pittsburgh with a degree in electrical engineering, Darragh has spent more than 20 years working in various fields in the construction industry.

Darragh's interest in the environment is tied to his roots growing up in Pittsburgh, Pennsylvania, where the booming industrial Pittsburgh was once described as "hell with the lid off." The subsequent collapse of the steel industry in the 1970s left the city economically and environmentally challenged and with huge health and social issues as well. The city has recovered to be one of the greenest in the country, but the tolls and stresses on families and the overall community during this period led Darragh to believe there had to be a better way. Since then, he has actively participated in numerous programs to advance sustainability issues and is also currently chair of MTS, the Institute for Market Transformation to Sustainability.

Stacy DeBroff, Chief Executive Officer and Founder, Mom Central, www.momcentral.com

In 1997, Mom Central chief executive officer and founder Stacy DeBroff left a successful career as a lawyer and founder of the public interest advising office at Harvard Law School to write books for parents and spend more time with her own two children, now ages 13 and 15. She went on to become a nationally acclaimed parenting expert and bestselling author of *The Mom Book Goes to School: Insider Tips to Ensure Your Child Thrives in Elementary and Middle School; SIGN ME UP! The Parent's Complete Guide to Sports, Activities, Music Lessons, Dance Classes, and Other Extracurriculars; The Mom Book: 4,278 of Mom Central's Tips for Moms from Moms;* and *Mom Central: The Ultimate Family Organizer.*

Through her parenting expertise, DeBroff has gained repeat invitations to share her down-to-earth point of view on national television shows, including NBC's *Today* show, CBS's *Early Show, Oxygen Live* with Gayle King, and *The Rachel Ray Show.*

Because of her unique and unprecedented mom reach, DeBroff has also been recruited by multiple national corporations in their pursuit of the mom market. She has worked with Whirlpool, Upromise, Neosporine, Pfizer, Kimberly-Clark, Office Depot, Swiffer, Kajeet, and Airborne as a spokesperson.

Mimi Doe, Author and Founder, www.SpiritualParenting.com
Mimi Doe is the author of five books: *Don't Worry: You'll Get In! Nurturing Your Teenager's Soul, Busy but Balanced: Practical and Inspirational Ways to Create a Calmer, Closer Family,* and *10 Principles for Spiritual Parenting,* which won a coveted Parents' Choice Seal of Approval and was honored as a finalist in the Books for a Better Life Award. *Ladies Home Journal* called Mimi a "parenting guru" and she has appeared on the *Oprah* show. She holds a master's degree in education from Harvard.

Doe is featured weekly on *New Morning TV,* airing on the Hallmark Channel, and was recently seen on the CBS *Early Show.* Her work has been covered in virtually every woman's magazine as well as top publications, including *Child, Parenting, McCalls, Family Circle, Redbook, Reader's Digest, Publisher's Weekly, USA Today,* the *Wall Street Journal,* the *Boston Globe,* the *London Independent,* and the *Washington Post.*

Doe has her finger on the pulse of what parents, in particular moms, care deeply about. Her popular online newsletter, "Spiritual Parenting Thought for the Week," has more than 50,000 subscribers from around the world. Doe is the mother of two children, ages 16 and 18, and lives in Concord, Massachusetts.

Amy Keroes, Founder and Chief Executive Officer, Mommytrackd.com
Amy Keroes received her undergraduate degree from Northwestern University and her law degree from the University of California–Los Angeles. She was a fifth-year associate at Latham & Watkins when she switched gears and took a position as senior corporate counsel for Gap Inc. She worked at Gap for six years, managing the company's intellectual property litigation and all marketing-related partnerships and promotions. Keroes managed celebrity advertising deals, including the contract

negotiations for Madonna, Missy Elliott, Sarah Jessica Parker, and Lenny Kravitz.

She lives in Mill Valley, California, with her husband, Jeff, her seven-year-old son Matty, and her four-year-old daughter Jessie.

Hedy Lukas, Vice President, Integrated Marketing Communications, Kimberly-Clark Corporation, www.kimberly-clark.com

Hedy Lukas is vice president of Integrated Marketing Communication (IMC) for Kimberly-Clark's North Atlantic (North America and Europe) Consumer Products group. Under her direction, the IMC team is accountable for the Integrated Marketing Planning for Kleenex, Huggies, Pull-Ups, Scott, Kotex, Poise, and Depend, as well as for other Kimberly-Clark brands and the execution and management of approximately $600 million in Media, Consumer Promotion, Relationship Marketing, Shopper Marketing, and Packaging Design.

Before joining Kimberly-Clark, Lukas was a partner in a regional advertising agency, served as assistant press secretary for a Wisconsin governor, and was a policy analyst in the Wisconsin Office of Federal-State Relations. Lukas has a graduate degree in public administration from the University of Wisconsin and an undergraduate degree in journalism.

Nan McCann, President, PME Enterprises, www.pme-events.com, www.m2w.biz, www.m2moms.com

As president of PME Enterprises, Nan McCann oversees the planning, development, and implementation of major conferences including M2W, the country's premier marketing to women event; M2Moms, the country's largest marketing to moms conference; and Good and Green, a green marketing conference.

McCann is a proven sales and marketing executive with a documented record of energizing businesses.

McCann's founding of PME evolved directly from her decade-long new business consultancy. Throughout the 1990s she provided both sales and marketing services to a wide range of clients such as Jim Henson Productions, MarketSource Corp., Modern Talking Pictures, Professional Team Publications, Key Productions, and Winstar Interactive Media Sales. At the same time, McCann was a featured monthly columnist for ABC Publishing's *Selling Magazine*. Prior to this, she held senior sales and marketing positions in target marketing (MarketSource Corp.), broadcasting (ABC and NBC Radio Networks), and advertising (Advertising Specialty Institute). McCann began her sales and marketing career by selling the importance of reading and writing to vocational education high school students.

Susan Molinari, Chair and Former Chief Executive Officer, The Washington Group; President, Ketchum Public Affairs, TWG, www.thewashingtongroup.com

The Honorable Susan Molinari is the former chair and chief executive officer of The Washington Group and president of Ketchum Public Affairs. A member of Congress from 1990 to 1997, Molinari quickly became "one of the most distinctive Members of the House" and "one of the most visible voices for her party," according to the authoritative *Almanac of American Politics*. As a result, after just four years in Washington and just weeks after the election of the first Republican House majority in 40 years, Molinari was elected by her colleagues to the eight-person Republican Majority Leadership, making her the highest-ranking woman in the Congress.

Before serving in Congress, Molinari was twice elected to the New York City Council, where she was Minority Leader. In 1997, she left Congress to co-anchor the team inaugurating CBS News Saturday Morning, where she conducted on-air interviews of national and international newsmakers. Today, Molinari is a regular contributor to CNBC's *Capital Report*. She is the co-author of the book *Representative Mom: Balancing Budgets, Bill, and Baby in the U.S. Congress* (Doubleday, 1998). She was chosen as *Glamour* magazine's Woman of the Year in 1996 and by *Time* magazine as 1 of 40 of the nation's most influential people under age 40 in the nation in 1994.

Molinari is married to former New York Congressman Bill Paxon, now a senior advisor at the law firm of Akin, Gump, Strauss, Hauer and Feld, and they have two daughters.

Paul Rand, President and Chief Executive Officer, Zócalo Group, www.zocalogroup.com

Paul Rand is responsible for overall client strategy and satisfaction as well as the leadership and growth of the Zócalo Group team. Prior to launching Zócalo Group, Rand served as a partner and global chief development and innovation officer at Ketchum, one of the world's leading public relations firms. Rand has 20 years of strategic communications experience, with expertise in corporate, industry analyst, financial, crisis, employee, business-to-business, media, and marketing communications. As the founder and chief executive officer of Corporate Technology Communications (CTC), he led CTC to becoming the Midwest's largest independent corporate and technology communications firm and among the most respected in the nation.

Rand serves on the executive committee and board for the Word of Mouth Marketing Association (WOMMA) and is widely regarded as a leading expert in word-of-mouth marketing and brand evangelism. He has served as an adjunct faculty member at DePaul University's Kellstadt Graduate School of Business, teaching strategic planning and entrepreneurship. He is currently on the executive committee of the Dean's Board of Advisors. Rand has been featured or quoted on word-of-mouth marketing, business, and communications issues in the media, including in the *Wall Street Journal*, the *New York Times, Business Week* magazine, *National Public Radio*, the *Chicago Tribune, PRWeek, AdWeek, Advertising Age*, and numerous other outlets.

Janet Riccio, Executive Vice President, Omnicom Group, Inc.; Chief Executive Officer, G23, www.omnicomgroup.com

The actualization of G23 is the result of Janet Riccio's determination of a gap in the marketplace's understanding of the female economy. In addition to leading G23, Riccio is responsible for the global oversight of one of Omnicom's largest clients, McDonald's. In this role, Riccio fosters and facilitates multiple agency collaboration, intercedes on behalf of both agencies and clients to develop solutions to any ongoing partnership issues, and taps into Omnicom specialist agencies to bring ideas unique to their discipline to the clients.

Over the course of Riccio's 25 years in advertising, her collaborative business style has taken her to more than 30 countries on behalf of her clients and forged a deep appreciation of how relationships with consumers build brands around the world. In addition to her work on behalf of her client's brands, Riccio is also passionate about philanthropy. An active adviser to the global Women's Funding Network, Riccio serves on the board of directors of the Make a Wish Foundation for Metro New York.

Rich Tavoletti, Director, Canned Food Alliance, www.mealtime.org

Rich Tavoletti is director of the American Iron and Steel Institute's (AISI) Container Market Program. He is also director of the Canned Food Alliance, a national consortium of steel producers, can manufacturers, and food processors that is increasing consumer awareness of the nutritional and convenience benefits of canned food.

Tavoletti joined AISI as marketing manager of market development in 2001 and is responsible for developing and implementing the AISI Market Development Strategic Plan to increase demand for tin mill products. He serves as liaison to the U.S. Department of Agriculture, where he represents the North American steel industry on issues relating to the Farm Bill, the Specialty Crop Block Grant, and the Women, Infants, and Children (WIC) food assistance program.

Tavoletti is a member of the Produce for Better Health Foundation's Communications Committee and the National Fruit and Vegetable Alliance. He holds a bachelor of science degree in marketing from Indiana University of Pennsylvania.